WOUNDED HEALERS

Reflections on 20 Years of Tumultuous
Membership of the Chiron Brotherhood -
A Men's Group for Male Healers

Written by the Founding Members
Farra Allen
Dennis McCauley
George Poirier
Gregory Possman
Colin Tipping
Jack Winner

Edited and Compiled by
Colin Tipping

Copyright © 2014, Colin C. Tipping

Wounded Healers
Reflections on 20 Years of Tumultuous Membership of the Chiron Brotherhood - A Men's Group for Male Healers

Written by the Founding Members
Farra Allen
Dennis McCauley
George Poirier
Gregory Possman
Colin Tipping
Jack Winner

Compiled by Colin Tipping
Published in January, 2015

Line Editing and Proof Reading by Shari Claire

ISBN 978-0-9821790-6-2

Global 13 Publications, Inc.
355 Ridge Hill Circle
Marietta, GA 30064

Printed in the United States of America

From the Left: Back Row: Jack, Gregory, Dennis.
Front Row: Colin, Farra, George, Gerry

i

This book is dedicated to
our respective partners all of
whom gave us unqualified support
for participating in this men's group
from it's very beginning and
continue to do so.

Contents

Preface

by Gregory Possman

For the first 40 years of my life I had chosen a lonely solitary path, walled off from the possibility of having any kind of intimacy with men. Through my experiences in the Chiron Brotherhood I realized I had a choice; the choice to experience acceptance, camaraderie, support and love from the male of the species.

I suspect there are many men (and women) who may not realize they have this same choice to experience these positive and very pleasant emotions. We do have a choice and we deserve to experience acceptance, camaraderie, support and love.

If we can blast through our beliefs, navigate through our fears and assert our deservability, we can choose to belong to a group where these feelings are abundant. I wanted to belong to something like this in my first 40 years, but I never felt it could happen.

Having joined groups, participating in athletics and trying hard to fit in, I never felt the level of participation and belonging, so earnestly desired that I feel in this Brotherhood. The chemistry was just not there.

Every man and woman deserves the opportunity to belong to something that gives meaning to their lives. The feelings that come with belonging to a group in which there is acceptance, non-judgment, unconditional support and gratitude can be experienced by anyone, male or female, by becoming a member of, or even creating, a gender-specific group similar in kind and intention to the one described in this book.

As you will see as you read on, the Chiron Brotherhood is a place to go where we can truly open up, tell the truth, be heard and express our concerns without fear of judgment. I hope it will provide a model for others to follow and emulate.

This book is a report of our experience over the 20 years of being together, beginning in 1994, to explore, to grow and to bare our souls. And we did all of that for the purpose of our own growth.

There was terror in the beginning for me due to my lack of trust of men. Men had always represented competition to me. Even when other men and I were supposedly on the same team, I always knew I was competing for a position on the team. There would always be a winner and a loser. The winners formed their own group and the losers, well you know the rest.

The Chiron Brotherhood never had winners and losers. We all won and we all grew. I want this book to introduce to everyone their opportunity to belong to a group where everyone is a winner. I deserve it and so do you.

Gregory A. Possman

INTRODUCTION

by Colin Tipping

How the Chiron Brotherhood came into being and why it did is something of a mystery in and of itself. There was definitely a lot of synchronicity involved which is always a clue that Spirit is heavily involved in causing something like this to occur.

As we look back now after 20 years, it is clear to us that there was a greater purpose in it. Of course, we did not know it in the beginning and never could have imagined us writing a book about it 20 years later.

When we came to realize what a powerful process we had created we felt the need to share it with the world, and over the years had made some attempts at doing so. But we had never found the right way to do it. A book—at this time, in 2014—seemed exactly right. As soon as it was suggested we all said, "Let's go for it!"

This was agreed in spite of the risk involved in putting ourselves out there and revealing our dark sides to the world. It seemed as though there was a spiritual imperative driving us to do it which we could not ignore.

We immediately conceived of it being a collaborative project with each of us contributing to it in our own way. As an established author and with experience in publishing books, I agreed to be the project leader.

It was quickly established that the core of the book would be —with the benefit of 20 years of hindsight—our own individual reflections on how it was for each of us to participate in this group experience year after year, and how it might have impacted our lives.

At one of our editorial meetings when we read our reflections to each other, it was agreed they should remain largely as written and minimally edited in order to maintain the authenticity of each offering. This would inevitably involve some repetition of facts and even some inconsistencies between the stories, but given that memory is selective and not always totally accurate that would be inevitable. I hope you, dear reader, will forgive us for that.

Like many events in life that turn out to be significant, it began as a conversation over dinner. In between mouthfuls, Dennis McCauley began telling George Poirier about a conversation he'd had with a mutual friend and acquaintance, Gregory Possman. He and Greg had attended a Men's Movement workshop in Greensboro, North Carolina, and while driving back from there had an interesting conversation.

The content of that conversation, as Dennis described it, lit a spark in George's mind that was to set off a chain of events that no one could have foreseen. On the drive home in the car, Dennis and Gregory had mused on the idea that there might be a need among men healers for a special kind of support group that would provide an opportunity to work on healing each other while at the same time addressing the problems that men healers face in their practices.

George's whole body exploded with excitement. He knew exactly what they were talking about. He understood the problems that male healers faced and was very aware they were not being talked about, much less being addressed. This represented an opportunity to get it out into the open.

He also knew that in order to do healing work on other people, it was necessary to have cleared one's own energy field of unresolved issues. Being a member of a group of healers each committed to doing the work would be the best way to do it.

A few day later, George asked Dennis to come over for lunch to talk more about this. They both agreed to put the idea into action. "Let's invite a bunch of male healers and see whether they would like to join a group," they said. So George invited Farra, Colin, Gerry and a couple of others he knew. Dennis invited Gregory. Others were invited as well. This was in November, 1994.

How Jack Winner came to be invited was pure synchronicity. George and Farra were enjoying being out on Lake Lanier in Farra's boat. Out of the blue comes this single scull occupied by a person they both knew well. Her name was Benita. Now, bear in mind this is a huge lake with over 500 miles of coastline. Yet there she was. She was very surprised to see them, having no idea whatsoever that Farra lived close by. She guided her scull over to them and said, "Follow me. There's someone I want you to meet. He has a house just around the bay from here."

They followed her lead and was duly introduced to Jack Winner. Having introduced them, Benita turned around and disappeared. George and Farra hit it off immediately with Jack and a few days later they invited him to be part of the group. He accepted.

All those who responded to the call gathered for the inaugural meeting of what was later to become the Chiron Brotherhood, at Farra's house on the Lake on November 18, 1994.

There were about a dozen present. There was plenty of enthusiasm, but in the end there were eight of us who said, "Let's do it." They were George Poirier, Farra Allen, Colin Tipping, Gregory Possman, Jack Winner, Gerry Parsons, Dennis McCauley and Joe Teagarden. You will get to meet the five who still meet on a regular basis in a moment as well as a contribution from Dennis, who stopped coming after a while for reasons he will explain.

After a lot of talk, we settled on the idea that we would meet once every six to eight weeks for a whole weekend, beginning on Friday evening and ending on Sunday afternoon. There would be no women present nor even in the vicinity. It had to be men only in the house.

At that point, the discussion turned to the purpose for the meetings and what the focus would be, at least to start with. It was agreed, that while a big part of it was to deal with the problems we faced as male healers in having to deal with needy and emotionally starved women, there was also the need

4

for us, as wounded healers to confront our shadow and heal our own deep personal wounds. This was to be the main focus.

This led us to adopt the name of "The Chiron Brotherhood." Chiron is the name given to a celestial body known as the "Asteroid of the Wounded Healer," so that made it the perfect name for us.

By doing this work on ourselves, we would be more effective as healers because we would cease projecting our own woundedness onto our clients. All too often therapists unconsciously project their own unhealed issues on their clients and, as a result, keep them addicted to victim consciousness. That's not therapy; it's abuse.

Right from the start, though, we recognized we would have to take this problem down into parts of ourselves we never had acknowledged or had allowed to surface before.

Nevertheless, everyone in the group knew and was dedicated to the notion that no stone was to be left unturned in our quest to heal our pain bodies and salvage our true selves from the rotting debris of at least some parts of our lives. It meant we had to be vulnerable with other men in a way that we might never have allowed ourselves to be before.

However, even though the sexuality issue was always there bubbling away on the back burner and was the subject of much discussion during our social time, the work focused almost exclusively on doing the deep healing work, each of us offering our various expertise in the healing arts to make it happen for whomever was willing to dig deep.

We would get together on Friday evening and that was social time. It would be time to catch up, swap stories, argue, eat dinner and hang out. That was always fun. Saturday evening was also social time and that always went into the early hours because we had so much to discuss.

Incidentally, thinking back now, I don't ever remember the issue being discussed whether alcohol or drugs should or should not be a part of it, even during our social time. Except for one time, quite recently in fact, when Jack and I did mushrooms while being fully supported by George and Farra, drugs and alcohol were never part of our group experience. The purpose for our meeting was to be more conscious than normal, not to numb out and be less than conscious. We didn't watch TV or movies for the same reason.

But come Saturday morning at 9:00 a.m. after clearing each other's energy by smudging with some burning sage, we would sit together on the floor in a tight circle holding hands while going into a deep meditation and, more often than not, receiving a channeling through Greg.

After that ritual, we would go to work. And we went at it like a pack of hungry hyenas—or pit bulls—take your pick.

Most of the time, we each had arrived with a personal issue to work on and whoever went first would put it out there, laid bare, raw and uncensored. The others would then dive in, pick at it like gulls over a landfill, trying to uncover the deep, dark issues lurking beneath that person's story, poking and prodding to find out what he might be hiding or avoiding. It was tough and uncompromising. Sometimes even brutal.

But, it was done with so much love and support that it did not feel like that.

We each knew it was essential in order to blast past the ego and break down the unconscious defense mechanisms preventing us from accessing what was really going on and what really needed to be healed.

Our commitment was to help each other bust through our stories and find the truth. For some in the group, it was about going in and accessing the pain of their childhood wound in order to heal it once and for all. We found we were able to do for each other in one or two hours what a conventional therapist would need years to achieve. But it was intense, to say the least.

It wasn't just verbal either. We were all used to doing bodywork of some kind, so we would get the person on a massage table or on the floor and really get into their body, using various techniques like Shiatsu, breathwork, massage and Reichian bodywork to break down the armoring around the heart, etc.

Just for the record, Jack was a certified chiropractor, Farra was a certified massage therapist who had co-founded and directed the Atlanta School of Massage, with his then recently divorced wife. George was a Shiatsu specialist, a Reichian bodyworker and a breathworker of the Holotropic variety which involved pushing acupuncture points to release held energy in certain areas of the body. That was my part, too. Gregory was as intuitive with that aspect as he was with all his work and was always right on the place that needed pressure.

7

Research shows that our stories about our wounds, disappointments, traumas, betrayals, abandonments etc., live on in our bodies as energy patterns. Bruce Lipton in his groundbreaking book, *The Biology of Belief,* showed that these stories are stored in our cellular structure. That's why this bodywork stuff was so important. It wasn't enough just to talk through our issues, we had to fully experience the pain of them in our bodies so those energy patterns could be released and new patterns created.

We would work in this way all day, with a brief respite for lunch, until about 6:00 p.m. Then we would all go out to dinner and talk until late into the evening. Come Sunday morning, we would go back to work again with much the same gusto as on Saturday.

When we were not focused on the healing work itself, there was a lot of clashing and jousting around logistics that would, in turn, bring up all sorts of male control issues among the biggest egos in the room. These issues would then become grist to the processing mill.

The main one from day one was the issue of commitment. We argued ad-infinitum about whether our commitment to this group had to be 100% or whether there would be some latitude about attendance.

George was the one who wanted it to be all or nothing, and he laid heavily into Joe who always wanted to find a way to be half in and half out. Dennis was another who wavered in his resolve to attend every meeting.

8

Farra, always the peacemaker and compromiser was less fixed about it and argued for a degree of latitude at least. Jack and I, as usual, said very little and did not express a high intention either way. Neither he nor I imagined the group would last that long anyway. And, come to that, I doubt the others did either. Certainly none of us would have put money on it lasting 20 years.

Eventually, George won the day and it was agreed that the meetings were to be a priority and we agreed we would stay for the whole weekend. I was glad in one sense because in the early days I had a lot of resistance to going each time and I knew that if there was some latitude about attending, I would take advantage of it—taking the path of least resistance.

So that was the process. And it carried on like that for many years. As we departed on Sunday afternoon, each of us felt we had achieved a lot of healing and felt excited about coming together again in a few weeks. It was like we were going down through the layers on each occasion that we met.

Nevertheless, looking back, it did seem we were going over the same stuff for a long time and it was that perception of being stuck that caused Jack to pull out in December, 1996. That was a big shock to the group and a great drama, but I will leave that event to be sliced and diced in each of our "Reflections" chapters in Part Two.

However, for all that we discussed our respective childhood experiences and current relationship issues, the underlying theme that began to drive the group discussion in the later years was sex addiction and the problems caused by that.

Four members of the long-term group would probably now, in retrospect, describe themselves as having a strong addiction to sex for most of the years we were meeting.

I will let them tell their own stories around this and how it created havoc in their private lives, but what was really scary for them was that it proving extremely problematic in their respective practices as healers. You will read more about this in Chapter 3. Only two of us, Jack and myself, seemed relatively free of this problem, but as we shall see, observing it in the others was to have meaning for us two in a very different ways. That was why we hung in there with them.

As I mentioned earlier, we were committed to total honesty and transparency, so exactly how this addictive sexual behavior was acted out in all aspects of their lives was shared openly and freely. Nothing was left unsaid or hidden. This kind of honesty and degree of vulnerability could never have been achieved in a co-ed group. The women would have killed us. But by then we had established so much trust we felt confident that it would never be shared. (It was breached once, but George will talk about that.)

So why let all this dirty wash hang out on the line now in this book, you might well ask? What purpose will it serve? I have already mentioned that we had come to feel that there was a spiritual imperative to it, but here are some other reasons why we felt driven to write this book and create a website that offers even more material.

Firstly, we hope this book might encourage more men to come together in groups like this to share their innermost fears, their dreams, their frustrations, their joys, their sexual issues and so on.

From an early age, boys, and men too, spend most of their time relating to women. Intimate sharing between men is rare which causes a lot of toxic energy to be held deep in the mind and body — the very stuff of heart attacks, hypertension, depression and cancer.

It would demonstrate to the world and to men in particular what a dedicated group of men can accomplish with the commitment and courage to face shadow issues head-on, supported by other men committed to doing the same in an atmosphere of mutual love and support. It would show men that their strength manifests to the degree to which they are willing to be vulnerable.

Secondly, the book would show how different people have different sexual personalities and that we can divide most people into two types, both of which vary greatly in their characteristics and manifest behavior. While women seem to be more aware of and talk with their friends about their own sexual personalities and read magazines like Cosmopolitan to find comparisons, men have no such equivalent. They just don't talk about it other than to brag or make jokes' but that's it, more or less.

The extremes of these two types were very evident in our group as you will see as you read their chapters. This was an example of perfect synchronicity in how the group came together. By having the contrast, it gives us a way to show the differences in a very stark but realistic way and to demonstrate

11

how difficult it is for the extreme of one type to understand or empathize with the other. Without this understanding, people experience a great deal of misunderstanding and a whole lot of pain.

I am hoping this will take away from at least half the male population the belief that there is something wrong with them. I think this belief was held by everyone in our group albeit for very different reasons. In our case, this emotional divide in terms of our respective sexual personalities was there for many years. We really did not understand each other for a long time. That's not to say, however, that this gulf is exclusive to men. It isn't. It occurs between male and female all the time, too, and accounts for why a lot of relationships fail.

This model of sexuality is outlined in Chapter 4, as the Preamble to Part Two so that you might see within each of our Reflections how it played out for each of us in our lives and in our relationships. You will also find a questionnaire in the Appendix, which you can fill out to see where you might be on the scale and where your partner might be.

This brings me to another good reason to share this information. Women will read this book too, and will get insights that they will find helpful in understanding their own sexual personality and how it relates to their partner's.

It has taken a long time to come to terms with our individual sexual personalities without making them wrong, but we have found that by sharing the differences in the group and seeing how these variations have affected our lives, we have come to understand more about the two main, radically different and in many ways totally opposite sexual personalities that exist within the population and, as a result, have been able to integrate more of the opposite into our own.

Jack and I were definitely representative of one extreme, while all the others, even those who are no longer with us today, having either left or died, occupied the other, albeit in varying degrees. This would account for why sex was the main pre-occupation for the whole group in the later years after all the power struggles had abated. That was because overt sexuality was not a major theme in Jack's or my life, but it was for the others, more or less, an obsession. It eventually came to dominate the discussion.

And, for me, that was OK, for as you will see as you read about the characteristics of each type in another chapter, sexuality is something my type processes mentally rather than emotionally so it was interesting and fascinating to watch the struggle it seemed to be for those of the opposite type and to compare it with my own approach to it.

Now, let's meet the members who are the remaining five who started the Chiron Brotherhood 20 years ago and the joint authors of this book. We are listed in first name alphabetical order.

Each one has written a short biography so you can get a brief sense of who we are. Bear in mind, though, you are going to know a lot more about us in Part Three once you read our reflections of how it was for us to be a member of this group.

Colin Tipping

 Born in England in 1941, I was raised by working-class parents. I had an elder brother and a younger sister. My parents were good people, loving and hard-working, and I consider myself blessed for having had a stable and enjoyable childhood.

Even as a boy, I seemed to inspire the trust of people who needed to talk about their feelings. I guess they found in me someone who would listen and not judge.

After a four-year stint in the Royal Air Force, and three years in the corporate world after that, I went back to college to train as a teacher at the age of 29, and was, by that time, a father of three wonderful children from my first wife. I then returned to the University to be a lecturer in Education and did that for ten years.

At the age of 43, after my second divorce, I immigrated to the United States in 1984. I became a clinical hypnotherapist and began practicing in Atlanta, Georgia.

I met JoAnn Shearer in 1989 and we married in 1990. She and I began doing cancer retreats in the North Georgia mountains. We realized that conventional forgiveness was never going to work with these folks, so that's when we created the approach which was to become Radical Forgiveness.

I wrote my first book, *Radical Forgiveness, Making Room for the Miracle* in 1997, and have been teaching it to people all around the world, with JoAnn, ever since.

14

In 2001, we founded the Institute for Radical Forgiveness Therapy and Coaching, Inc., based in Atlanta, Georgia. The Institute continues to this day to train and certify professional Radical Living Coaches and Radical Forgiveness Therapy Practitioners in the U.S. and around the world.

Farra Allen

 I was born an only child in Northern Kentucky. My parents were both school teachers. We grew up in a suburban setting that was very idyllic. When I was seven years old, my father contracted polio and was severely crippled. His frustration at being no longer able to coach track and gymnastics turned to rage and he became a rageaholic.

My need to please him and my inability to fix him has been the main issue I have had to deal with all my life.

We were middle class whereas most all my classmates were very upper class. My best friend had a live-in maid who prepared all the meals, etc. They all belonged to the Country Club and had so much of what I wanted in life. In high school, I was a good athlete and student. I played varsity football, basketball, swimming and tennis. I wanted to be a football coach but was convinced to *supposedly* do more with my life. So, I went instead to a liberal arts college majoring in Psychology. After graduating, having grown up playing with soldiers, I wanted to be a Navy Seal. With the body bags coming back from Vietnam, my parents talked me into going to Grad School. I graduated from Law School and yet had no desire to become a lawyer. Instead, I became a massage therapist, taught massage, created the first massage school in the Southeast outside of Florida, and later went back to grad school to get a Master's Degree in Psychology and Counseling. In 1994 I became a Personal Coach and started LifeWorks School of Coaching which flourishes to this day and is my passion.

Along the way I was married twice, once for 7 years and the second for 14 years. I was blessed with a son during my first marriage. My current partner and I have been together for now 14+ years and we are very happy and support each other's dreams.

George Poirier

I was born in 1948, the firstborn of a Catholic family in New England. I am the oldest of eight children.

I arrived with a Type A personality. I had enormous energy and was running everywhere I went. Hyperactive would be a good word to describe me. I loved sports.

I was a good student and well-educated, and left home to marry my pregnant girlfriend at the age of 20. I went from being a student and musician to the breadwinner of a young family in the twinkling of an eye. Quite a shock!

Having a natural ability as a salesman, I embarked on a career in direct sales and later created several small businesses. This was a very intense lifestyle.

After 20 years of business and going through three marriages, I had a life-changing experience during a weekend workshop I attended in July, 1988. This led me into Reiki training. Two years later, I became a Shiatsu practitioner and later studied Reichian bodywork.

I then developed my own body-mind-therapy method. After exploring several psycho-spiritual traditions around the world, I developed the dynamic technique that maximized the experience for my clients. I would challenge my clients to break through self-imposed limitations and step into their personal power. With compassion, empathy and tough love, I encouraged and stimulated their personal growth and spiritual development.

I am an extroverted and articulate person. I enjoy intellectual stimulation. I read voraciously and enjoy researching human potential on any level. I am nurturing and enjoy giving of myself to family and friends. I crave peace and solitude and at this time, I have a lot of both in my life. I am very grateful.

Gregory Possman

I am a psychic trance channel. I'm not altogether comfortable with it, but I offer it as a service to people and bring forth a number of entities from the spiritual realm to give advice to people. I also conduct workshops during which they come through me to relate to those present.

Besides the U.S., I work a lot in Denmark and have a strong following there.

In my younger days, I spent the winters snow skiing, hiking, hunting, and shoveling snow. My summers were spent cutting wood, trekking through the forest, swimming, walking and motorcycling.

I've been blessed with two wives in this life, both older than I. Most of my friends, with a few exceptions, are older than I am as well. I have three children from my first marriage.

My belief in reincarnation has made losing loved ones easier, but not easy. Though I try to minimize my complaining about life, and don't always understand it, I do believe there is perfect order in the universe.

Accepting life's idiosyncrasies and outcomes are much more important than understanding them. This has allowed me to enjoy greater balance and more inner peace in my life than ever before.

I am solution oriented so I am often described as being wise, responsible, organized and efficient. Some see me as aloof, uncaring and distant. I try not to be.

As an ordained minister, with a successful wedding practice, a family, and business to run, social skills are important to me. Even as a trance channel, I sometimes refrain from adding my two cents worth for fear it will be rejected or I'll be judged.

I am an optimistic man who tries to choose kindness, compassion, tolerance and understanding rather than fear and despondency. I do not always succeed but sufficient perhaps to make a difference in the lives of others. That's why I'm here.

Jack Winner

 I am an introvert by nature. I think of myself as being, not so much shy as somewhat naive and ill-informed, especially when it comes to things like money, sex, politics, religion and even relationships. Outwardly, I might seem to be relating well but inside I often feel like I want to go off and hide, just to be alone. That's where I am the happiest.

I think others see me as self-confident, focused, certainly passionate and motivated. But the truth is I am someone who talks excessively fast, without pronouncing my words such that people have difficulty understanding me.

When I was in front of someone or a group of intelligent—aware people, I would fear for what I'd say and if what I said was really appropriate in the conversation.

I wanted to be part of this men's group because they felt like kindred spirits. But, the acceptance I wanted was not for me, not just my personality. It was for me, or the 'I' in me, that I wanted this group and myself to acknowledge. I knew there was a deeper richer purpose to be here, I just couldn't find it in what everyone else said was life, as we know it.

My inability to communicate was probably my biggest challenge and burden. Not only could I not formulate supportive and constructive thoughts to others, I couldn't express them where they could support or embrace 'me' with them.

I found if I looked good, color coordinated my clothes or in general stayed in control I could orchestrate myself to be socially acceptable. This was exhausting most of the time, yet it seemed to work.

The real me wanted to have a conversation, a relationship with the real you. Not the superficial you … your money, your car, your golf clubs, your sexual activities. The *real* you. That's who I was and that's who I wanted to be with. Anything else was wasted conversation.

I am pleased and privileged to be writing this book with my brothers because we are kindred spirits.

It has been interesting to me that for the on and off twenty years we have been together I never really thought of any one of these guys as my close personal friends outside of our weekends together.

Except for then, I didn't hang out with them except for a few exceptions. I didn't call and /or talk for long periods of time. Never played golf, shared, traveled with them or their wives. Never felt like I really wanted to. But I wouldn't miss a weekend with them. Wouldn't think of it. I trust each one with my physical life and my spiritual life. I would liken it to the bonds formed in the military between comrades. That situation did not happen for me. But, I still wanted to bond with someone or some others who could understand *me*. I wanted to be relevant and I did not want to leave this earth plane without somebody knowing who I was.

My hope is that there are other men, and maybe women, who know they are not complete and would like some insights as to how they might make that happen. This is how it happened for me, just maybe our experiences might help you realize your completeness.

PART ONE

SETTING THE STAGE

Chapter 1. *Wounded Healers*
by George Poirier

Chapter 2. *Understanding Our Sexual Personality*
by Colin Tipping

Chapter 3. *The Male Healer's Minefield*
by Gregory Possman, George Poirier and
Colin Tipping

Chapter 1:
Wounded Healers and the Primal Wound
by George Poirier and Farra Allen

W e chose the name *The Chiron Brotherhood* because in Greek mythology, Chiron is the archetype of the wounded healer. Carl Jung coined the term *wounded healer* to express the concept that a healer must confront his own wounds in order to receive the gift of healing for himself and others. It's an alchemical term that we were deeply committed to in the context of this group. Again, not something that men, as a general rule, normally gravitate to. Nonetheless, the core of our group remained committed to the concept for 20 years.

Embracing the wound is not a one-time event. It's a dynamic process that unfolds in a way that reveals something deeply buried within ourselves. It's the opposite of repression and denial. However, going through and embracing the woundedness is very much an initiatory experience that leads to oneness and wholeness.

The ego expresses this as a sort of death. It's a journey that leads us to something within ourselves that unleashes a psychic transformation. It's an awakening to something greater within ourselves.

In the group, we all reflected aspects of ourselves that were hidden and repressed. This allowed us to embrace and process these deep-seated wounds. We always had the awareness that the work we were doing within the context of the group was facilitating something in the collective. Exactly what, we never knew. We felt that as we heal ourselves, we heal the world. Taking the process from the personal to the collective helped facilitate the integration process for all of us. We were all committed to being messengers of consciousness expansion in the world and the most effective way of accomplishing this was to keep focusing on ourselves; a holographic or hermetic approach to healing. As above, so below.

Continuing to focus on this inner world, we discovered that what made our wounds real was our own imagination. This insight allowed us to see our wounds as impermanent. Consequently, we are able to re-create the wound into an empowering resource that we could apply in our lives and share with others. While our wounds felt personal, our group process was transpersonal and universal. It was from this transpersonal realm that the healing took place. In this way, the wound became an opportunity for transformation.

At birth, we're thrown into a world that is strange and unfamiliar to us. Suddenly separated from our mother's womb, we are immediately confronted with our own mortality and anxiety over survival. We totally forget what we are is a conscious eternal being. We become identified as a mortal being and perceive life through our not yet developed five senses. Quite a shock indeed.

Anyone who has experienced conscious connected breath-work, rebirthing, or Holotropic breathwork has re-experienced this birthing trauma. This trauma is reinforced with the conditioning we received by our family and society that leads us to create a personality/ego which is carefully constructed to erect a protective psychological wall for us to exist within.

Denial of our mortality seems to be a strategy of the ego. After all, if we are born to die, what's the point of being alive. The existential dilemma. However, this expression of our mortality is the basis for the primal wound; a dualism between our conscious soul in our mortal bodies. This duality between mortality of the body and the immortality of consciousness sets up all sorts of pathological complexes. We spend the rest of our lives trying to psychologically survive in our own skin. If I'm an immortal soul what am I doing in this decaying body? What's the point? Our search for meaning becomes the reason to be alive, for as long as these bodies exist.

As children, we're pretty much told about our purpose in life. Be a good boy, behave and get good grades, make Mommy and Daddy proud. Pleasing our parents and authority figures are paramount. In my family system, I was the oldest of the children. My assigned role was to be the protector of my younger siblings. As I got older and my father spent more time away from the family, that included being emotional support to my mother. To the degree that I missed the mark was the degree that I was not enough and reprimanded, sometimes severely. This led to all measure of suppression that got acted out as rage towards my brothers, fights with my friends and cutting up in school.

It wasn't until I was in my late 20s that I started asking myself the philosophical questions of what's the point of all this. Life seemed like a never-ending merry-go-round of seeking more and more, yet feeling less fulfilled. I had achieved much of what I dreamed of financially, maritally, and the accumulation of various toys, but still felt empty. It wasn't until age 40, when my life crashed down around my ears, that I was ready to look inside myself. What I discovered was a deeply wounded and repressed child that never developed a healthy way to processes feelings and emotions.

The turning point was when I went from having my prime purpose of making money to exploring my inner psyche and consciousness. This led me on a 25-year journey of peeling off layers of repressed energy and allowing my inner self to shine through. But as this process continues, my inner self is tossed back upon itself as it seeks meaning and value. In the past, meaning was not discovered but instilled in me by others. Values are totally reinterpreted. It's time to stand autonomously. As Nietzsche would say:

> "The world's a gate
> To deserts stretching mute and chill
> Who once was lost
> What thou has lost stands nowhere still."

This is the moment of surrender, where the ego allows the spirit and intuition to move through life, embracing the Taoist tradition of *wu wei* where one goes through life without effort, without intention and from the heart. This transforms oneself from service to self, to service to others.

The savior archetype seems to be a complex that I adopted at age three, when my six-month-old infant brother died unexpectedly. My memory is of deep sadness in my parents and young brother. My response was that to survive in my family system, I had to be the emotional caretaker to my parents and siblings. I've been acting out this complex all of my life. While this dynamic has proceeded from deep in the subconscious, I have struggled with it and developed a love/hate relationship with it.

Women I've been in relationships with have experienced both sides of this complex. When I love myself, they experience the loving/nurturing side of my personality. When I hate myself, the hateful side of my personality, traditionally results in my sexually acting out.

Having spent years processing all the guilt and shame associated with the negative side of this complex, I've arrived at a place of peace within myself, and am able to share that with my partner and those whose lives I touch.

The savior complex is still strong in me as it has been recently triggered by the knowledge of my closest brother being diagnosed with a tumor on his liver. All the old terror of losing my family is present, and it's all about how I can protect my family from the emotional pain and help heal my brother.

This savior complex that I created at age three as a survival strategy has actually separated me psychologically from the intense loving connection I experienced with my mother at birth. I spent 47 years of my life attempting to re-experience that connection while acting out a complex that has kept me separated from it. This would be the progression of my primal wound.

George, June 2014

As George points out, our initial wounding occurs even prior to our *heads popping out* here on planet Earth. In the prenatal stage, we are at the height of our sensitivity and our radar is picking up on every nuance, especially our birth Mother's feelings and emotions as she goes through her pregnancy. If she and our father are emotionally involved in any upsetting circumstances......we feel it.

It feeds the primary fear of survival we begin to feel just prior to coming out of the birth canal and adds to the shock of emerging from the safe harbor of Mum's womb into a world of change and uncertainty. BAM! It hits us and everything after that is merely a *stack attack* on top of that, which reinforces and reminds us of the primal wounding. What a way to enter!

This is how this showed up for me. My mother had 3 miscarriages prior to becoming pregnant with me. She was getting older and she was told this was her last chance at having her first and only baby.

Needless to say, both my parents wanted this to happen in a very big way, so the pressure was on. I felt this in the womb and to prove it I came out with both fingers curled up and my toes so curled together that my father told me he had to massage them on a daily basis to get them to straighten out somewhat. To this day my two smallest toes are both mildly curled under and I still clench my fists creating tension in my hands. (No accident that I created the Atlanta School of Massage.)

So, I was a Godsend and as such my Mom would enter statistics of all kinds into a baby book of my first seven years. This was extensive as were her attention to me and we connected strongly. Feeling this connection along with the glee of my father finally getting the child he wanted and the elation of it being a boy (he was a track, gymnastics, and football coach), left me smiling continuously. So, when the first smack of my father's outstretched hand hit my face I was catapulted back into my initial wounding and it went on from there.

Even to this day when I do something that does not meet approval of another, especially those close to me, I shudder. I loved the adoration and seek to recreate it wherever and whenever I can.

This has created co-dependency issues for me to deal with. Most especially I developed an unusually intense bond with my Mother. As I have mentioned elsewhere, I formed an Oedipal complex with Mom. When my father saw this, he became extremely angry which caused my mother to withdraw from me. That, in turn, caused Dad to withdraw and become competitive with me. This was traumatic for me and it has taken me years to recover.

I have never really stopped needing to regain the bond and deep connection I had with my mother. Looking back I now see that I was constantly trying to re-create it by having sex with many women. This became overly important to me and occupied much of my waking time. I was constantly thinking and planning how to get back to a semblance of the feeling of the long gone connection and fulfillment that I had once felt with and for my mother.

This was how my primal wounding played itself out, not just in my childhood but all through my life. It was always an unconscious reminder of my initial wounding. Perhaps now you will be able to see how you might have repeated your primal wound over and over throughout your life

Possibly the greater the wounding afterward, the more one goes into denial and begins *acting out*. Much of today's pain inflicted upon others may, in fact, be inextricably tied to this initial wounding and the subsequent reminders.

Depending upon our individual interpretations and assessments of that which has occurred to us, we become angry and even rageful. Certainly this was the case for me and, I dare say, the case for so many men and women who seek to get back to that initial adoration they felt or wanted to feel.

This driving force coming from a place of deep and unconscious need can cause havoc and much damage if not met in some way.

An unmet need for approval and acceptance from our family of origin can create a deep wound which we act out in many different ways. I was very creative and always thinking outside the box but my father gave me a hard time about this. He would also tell me how I should have done something different versus whatever I did. He thought this was his job as a good father. However, for me it led me to believe deep down that there was something wrong with me and I could never make the right decision. To this very day I am hesitant to make decisions and though I have improved, it remains difficult for me.

Having shared my early wounding and how it has shaped my life, I invite you to look at how you may have experienced something similar. This may well account for how your life has turned out, how it has affected you and those around you, especially those closest to you.

This wounding is real and when the incidents that occur in our lives trigger it, we are off and running. It may not be pretty. Again, each of us has our version and the affect varies. Nevertheless, it is there and often much alive to this very day. Check it out by thinking about what it may be for you?

I know for myself, the fear of big change is strong and one of our greatest stressors. Even if it is a positive change, change in and of itself is threatening and now I see why.

The progression of this dynamic is real and in many cases continues to go on today. Consider how a seemingly small incident can cause one to react violently and totally inconsistent with the causal factor itself. Since we are tied to our subconscious belief system, we have inappropriate reactions which turn out to be destructive to all involved. As we go about life, we are now approaching each encounter with new eyes. We carry with it our old stories and wreak havoc upon others and ourselves as a result.

The healing of these primal wounds comes first from the awareness of what is actually in play for all of us. We must recognize and own that each of us has these wounds and we are all dealing with them to varying degrees as of this very day.

As we accept this with new understanding, and cease to act out in inappropriate and hurtful ways, we begin to heal. Furthermore, as we are aware of these wounds we can use varying methods of healing them including coaching, body/mind integration work and other modalities.

Creating new pathways once we understand the origin of our wounding will, in fact, lead us down the path of healing. To some degree it involves accepting the fact that this is something we will need to accept on a regular basis as an integral part of who we are and continue to be.

Farra, June, 2014

Chapter 2:
Understanding Your Sexual Personality
by Colin Tipping

In the Introduction, I pointed out that within the group there was a clear example of there being two types of sexual personality. Jack and I qualify as being classic examples of one type and George, Gregory and Farra being examples of the other, along with Gerry and Joe when they were there. Dennis was probably somewhere in between, but I'm not sure.

This information is important because it will have a bearing on everything else that follows in this book, particularly in regard to each of the brother's stories and reflections which they will be sharing in the following chapters.

The model I am about to share was created by John Kappas, Ph.D., the founder of the Hypnosis Motivation Institute and author of a number of books on hypnotherapy. I trained as a hypnotherapist under him at his school and have found this model to be extremely helpful in relationship therapy.

Through many years of doing relationship work with hundreds of couples, including many famous film stars, Kappas observed that there are basically two types of sexual personality, each driven by a specific fear.

35

On one side of the scale is the one he describes as *physical sexual.* On the other is one described as *emotional sexual.*

We need to be careful here, for the terms *physical sexual* and *emotional sexual* can be misleading. What is being referred to is how the person *defends* the part of themselves they feel to be most threatened.

The physical sexual is driven by an intense fear of rejection. Feeling vulnerable emotionally he or she defends against the threat of rejection by putting his/her physical body out front as a form of protection. The emotional sexual, on the other hand, is driven by a strong fear of intimacy. Feeling vulnerable physically, he or she protects his or her body by putting up a wall of emotion that comprises a mixture of fear, intense shyness and distrust.

This has all sorts of ramifications for how they each show up in the world. So let me provide a sketched profile of each extreme so you can determine where on the following scale you might be. The ideal is to have around a 60/40 bias towards one end or the other. That way you will be more able to understand those with the opposite bias.

As to how the current group members of the group stack up, George, Farra and Greg would be characterized as high physicals, while Jack and I would show up as being high emotionals.

Let me give you the typical characteristics of each (extreme) type as defined by Kappas. In the Appendix at the back of the book, you will find a questionnaire you can use to estimate where on the scale you might be.

People with an Extreme 'Physical Sexual' Personality

— They are classic extroverts who project their sexuality outwards, almost to the point of flaunting it.

— They are very comfortable with their bodies and have a high sex drive. They are ready for sex at a moment's notice and the men can last for hours.

— They wear clothes and jewelry that emphasize and bring attention to their physical body and their sexual attractiveness. This applies to women more than men, but a physical male is always conscious of how he looks.

— Image and appearance are very important to them. No matter what they buy, the main consideration is how it makes them look. They go for elegance, style, color, glitz, etc. They would never buy a car on the basis of fuel efficiency over style.

— They crave acceptance and attention because of their fear of rejection, which means everything they do is designed to get approval. They are extremely sensitive to criticism.

— When in conversation with you they will stand close, lock eyes and scan your face for the least sign of a possible rejection.

— If rejected, rather than withdraw, they will push forward even more, trying to win you over with charm and persuasion. They become very insistent and pushy. They will not take no for an answer, especially from an emotional sexual person of the opposite sex, to whom they are irresistibly attracted. They can be assertive and controlling, almost to the point of being obnoxious if they smell rejection.

— They are the life-and-soul of any party, very popular and always seem comfortable in social situations. They are never at a loss for something to talk about and small talk comes easy to them.

— They are natural risk takers in all aspects of their lives so they are often entrepreneurs and/or indulge in very physical sports, especially team sports.

— They are less concerned about their bodies being hurt than they are about having their feelings crushed.

— All their emotions are experienced physically rather than mentally, and when their feelings are hurt, they feel it as intense pain in their bodies. The pain can be so bad that they can literally be incapacitated by it for long periods of time.

— When a relationship ends they are devastated and have a very difficult time letting go of it. They take it very person-ally and feel utterly rejected. They also have a very hard time replacing. It may be many months before they will have another serious relationship, though they will have plenty of sex in the meanwhile. They need it just to feel OK.

— They are hopelessly idealistic about love and relationships and very romantically inclined. Once in a relationship they tend to be loyal and monogamous. At the same time, they are very jealous and possessive.

— They enjoy children and are very strong on family. They put family and/or relationships before career or any other aspect of life. It's their #1 priority.

— They communicate by indirect implication and inferences, relying on the listener to make the correct interpretation. On the other hand, they hear only what is said literally and don't pick up on inferences. You have to tell them explicitly and frequently that you love them. They will not infer that you do just because you are there.

People with an Extreme 'Emotional Sexual' Personality

— They are the classic introverts and they tend to fold down and withdraw into themselves to protect their feelings of physical vulnerability.

— They are not in the least bit comfortable in their bodies and have a closed, protective bodily stance that says, "Don't come close, and don't touch me." Their arms will be in front of them as protection and their feet tend to be turned inwards.

— They dress conservatively to divert attention away from their body and to hide their sexuality. Women will wear high neck dresses or loose clothing to hide their figure. They will wear minimal makeup, if they wear any at all, and will wear sensible shoes. Men will dress conservatively.

— The are not particularly social and have great difficulty making small talk. At parties, they are, usually, the wallflowers. They leave early.

— They feel their feelings inwardly and process them mentally. They seldom express feelings outwardly and do not like to show physical affection in public.

— They do not much like to be touched. Even a light touch quickly turns to irritation. The kind of touch a physical considers affectionate can seem like physical assault to an emotional.

— They are turned on sexually much more by visual and mental stimuli than by touch. They are not automatically ready for sex like the physical is and need a lot of warming up. Emotional men are not the sexual athletes physical sexual men are. Once they have ejaculated, it is all over, whereas physicals can go on for hours.

— For them, sex is not a high priority, neither is family, children or relationships. Their priority is work and career, followed by their hobby. Relationships come a distant third. They are not very fond of children and they may never choose to marry.

— They often have extramarital affairs and think little of it because they do not equate love with sex as does the physical. They like the mental excitement of an affair.

— When a relationship ends they get over it in a matter of days and replace easily. They do not take it as a personal rejection of themselves.

— They don't like team sports but they excel at individual sports that require rigorous training and are self-challenging.

— They lead with their minds in everything, from work, games and even sex. They are analytical, careful and methodical and therefore seldom spontaneous.

— They buy cars not on style and image but on which is the most efficient and best engineered. They will research it to death before they buy.

— If they go into business for themselves, they tend to be accountants, computer programmers, engineers, researchers, and technicians. They like precise, solitary work and are detail oriented. They can be very successful in business.

— They pick up on inferences and subtle implications, but they speak very directly and precisely. They don't waste words and are not physically expressive.

So there you have it. Not every one of these apply to the brothers, but from a broad brush point of view you will certainly get a better understanding of each of our stories in the following chapters if you use these as reference points.

I can't leave this conversation without explaining how this dynamic plays out in relationships, especially if one or both partners are at the extreme end of the scale. As you might imagine, initially, the opposites attract. A high physical will attract a high emotional and vice versa.

At a party, a high physical male will make a beeline for the retiring little emotional who is in the corner clutching her drink and looking shy and embarrassed. He desperately wants to rescue her and *bring her out*. She is initially turned off by him because he's so pushy, but eventually succumbs to his irresistible charm and his *take charge* attitude.

Communication seems to flow easily between them as well. That's because the physical speaks inferentially to the emotional who easily picks up on subtle implications of what is being said.

Conversely, the emotional speaks directly to the physical who likes direct communication, not inferences. The emotional says little but is a good listener, whereas the physical loves to dominate the conversation and is more than happy to have someone who will just listen. It seems like a match made in heaven.

Not only does the communication seem great during the honeymoon period, which lasts about six months, the emotional tends to act just like a physical in bed. So everything seems wonderful and the physical is convinced he or she has found a soul mate.

However, at around six months, each one begins reverting to their natural type. As the chemistry that enabled them to let down their defenses for a while begins to slowly fade, so their defenses re-emerge and their primary behavior comes to the fore again.

Consequently, emotionals begin withdrawing emotionally and wanting less sex. Their fear of intimacy and their tendency to avoid it returns. They begin focusing on things that interest them besides the relationship, such as their work or their hobby.

This drives the physical crazy because he or she interprets the emotional's behavior as an implicit rejection and an indication of their partner falling out of love. That makes him or her even more demanding of love, sex and physical affection, which in turn makes the emotional withdraw even more.

Once both fear responses have kicked in, the situation goes from bad to worse and the relationship is virtually irretrievable. If they stay together, it will be the emotional who will control relationship. That's because the physical will sell a large chunk of himself or herself in order to get whatever sex or physical affection the emotional is willing to give.

That's why a lot of strong-looking physical males are controlled by weaker-looking wives. A woman who knows how to manipulate that fear of rejection owns him.

You might imagine that the ideal arrangement would be two of the same together. This is not so.

Two physicals together would be in competition with each other and would act like a couple of divas. They would talk at each other in inferences with neither one of them picking up on them. They would be talking over each other and always seeing rejection in every utterance. It would be an intensely sexual liaison, but their jealousy and possessiveness would create terrible problems. They would always be fighting. Elizabeth Taylor and Richard Burton were good examples and this, and look what happened to them.

Two emotionals together would soon get very bored with each other. Sex would be nonexistent and their communications minimal. Their best chance at survival would be if they were to work together. Otherwise, they would be out looking for an affair just to relieve the boredom.

Concluding this discussion on the sexual self, a word of caution if I may. Remember that these are the extremes. Most of us are either predominantly physical or emotional but have enough of the other to balance it out to a greater or lesser degree. Perhaps more importantly, it helps to be able to understand your partner and realize that his or her behavior is normal for them. Get used to it.

Chapter 3:
The Male Healer's Minefield
As Seen Through the Eyes of Gregory,
George and Colin

Preamble: *All the way through this book you will see that the likelihood of sexual energy being present in the relationship between a male healer and a female client is a challenge for both. This was more of a problem for some members of the group than others. In each case it was handled differently depending on which end of the scale they sat. In this chapter, as men who are high on the physical sexual side, Gregory and George offer their personal reflections on how they handled it over time. Colin reflects how it was for him as someone relatively high on the emotional scale.*

Gregory's Viewpoint

At the time I entered into the alternative therapy field, I was in the middle of a nasty divorce and my life was in turmoil. I was also searching for something meaningful in the way of work.

I realized I had a gift for connecting with spirit beings on the other side of the veil. I was eager to offer my services as a conscious and psychic trance channel. I had also been introduced to a number of other alternative therapies and found an affinity for doing hands-on healing work in addition to the channeling. I still do both kinds of work in my practice.

Like many others doing *healing* work with people, becoming a Minister seemed as though it would protect me and allow me to work legally. I have since learned that it provides no real legal protection. Nevertheless, since a lot of people believe it does, then putting Reverend in front of one's name creates the illusion of it being *legal*. I've never been questioned in over twenty years of 'hands on' healing work with both males and females.

Immediately my work began attracting women whose challenges included unhappy relationships or marriages. Given my own addiction to sex and my admittedly good looks, I sensed this could be a problem for me.

I was aware of how common it was for women to be abused by therapists, shamans, and gurus and I did not want to join that club of abusers. That would have made me part of the problem, rather than part of the solution.

I was also aware of how a needy woman who craved intimacy would be easily attracted to a male who was sensitive to her emotions and was prepared to listen to her, and to interpret that as attraction. Seduction then was always a possibility and something to watch out for.

I learned very early that if a woman were to show signs of developing a romantic interest in me, any hope of remaining her therapist would have to be abandoned.

I knew other healers, even in our own group, who believed their client base was a healthy source for romantic indulgence. Though I disagreed, I seldom gave any advice as I knew it would not be well received. I could see that these indulgences could lead to confrontations with ex-partners or current partners of these individuals threatening the therapist with violent retribution, not to mention lawsuits. This is aside from the wrath of a rejected woman.

I was surprised not to have heard of more such encounters with the healers I knew. It would seem to me that at least one or two of these angry partners would have struck out and made good on their threat. Even so, I imagine that this had probably happened to others. A jealous man is a dangerous animal.

I did hear of at least one incident where a woman's teacher had shown interest in her and the husband threatened both legal action and violence. To my knowledge, neither occurred. Apparently the angered husband had his own career to protect.

I did have romantic relationships with three women I had met in the spiritual community in which I'd become involved. Two of these women were attendees at some of the groups I had channeled for. Although these women were not individual clients of mine, in retrospect, the ensuing relationships could be seen as unethical. Since I have little information about the gossip spread about me, I am unsure whether these relationships were seen by others as unprofessional or not. Though I would prefer to think they were not, I'm not sure in my own mind whether I had crossed a line.

The third woman I fell in love with, and I married. She had been a client, had become a friend, and as soon as we acknowledged our romantic interest in one another, the client role ended. By that time, I was clear as to what was ethical and what wasn't. We met in 1991 and are together to this day.

47

I am convinced that the personal information told to me by healers who were unethical in this regard, or from clients who were abused by their therapists, were lessons or warnings for me in disguise. Two possibilities existed:

1. The Universe (my higher self) was warning me not to go down a similar path.

2. I had completed that lesson and was now qualified to offer counsel or advice in that particular area.

Both are mirrors for all of us, reflecting a message, cosmic 2 x 4, or alarm that we need to pay attention to. Over the years, operating in integrity has paid off.

I have seen many very attractive clients and though temptation may have been there, as a force of habit, I must remind myself the purpose of our encounter and remain professional. Flirting of any form is unacceptable under such circumstances. Inappropriate familiarity is easily misunderstood.

In our minds, fantasy is always controllable. In reality, as opposed to fantasy, events can be completely misinterpreted and become not only dangerous but costly. I can only determine what appropriate behavior is for me. Each individual must choose what feels right for them. I would hate to go to sleep at night wondering if my activities throughout the course of my career were going to come back to haunt me. Thankfully, I'm confident they will not.

George's Viewpoint

Little did I know in 1988, the challenges I would be confronted with on my path as a male healer. The first was the personal *baggage* and propensities that I brought with me into this new and unfamiliar world.

The initial modality that I was trained in was Reiki. Although I would say that my Reiki Master was competent, her focus for me around personal boundaries was concentrated on how to protect myself energetically in my practice of Reiki. Included in this instruction was the boundaries concerning what was appropriate or inappropriate in proceeding with distance healing; all good counsel. Yet training in Reiki, Shiatsu or other trainings were deficient in preparing me for all the issues with which I was soon to be overwhelmed.

I was left to myself to deal with these issues as they arose. To say that I was unprepared to deal with them would be an understatement.

To put these challenges in some sort of historical perspective, at the time that I embarked on my new career, the New Age Movement was exploding. This movement was disproportionately populated with women. Many of these women were desperate to find a *spiritual* man to be in a relationship with. Needless to say, male healers were of particular interest to these ladies.

To add to my challenge, the number one issue that I dealt with for most of these women was their obsession with finding a relationship. Many times, I became the target of that projection and transference. I was also involved in multiple energetic practices aimed at developing Kundalini to perfect the light body.

My promiscuous past only added fuel to the fire. In addition, the primary healing modality was Reichian Bodywork. Deep psychological work where touch is involved, making the practitioner prone to being infected with the clients wounds or having one's wounds being re-activated.

The first three years were not much of a challenge for me, as I was developing my practice with only a few clients. In early 1991, I attended a sharing conference in North Georgia. This event was attended by other New Age types from around the U.S. When I walked into this conference, something ignited in me that's very difficult to describe. I barely slept for five days. From that weekend forward, these metaphysically oriented women were attracted to me like bees to honey.

From then on, I was challenged to attempt to manage and make sense of it all. To say that I was unprepared would be an understatement. It was during this weekend that two women from south Florida decided to sponsor my work. My practice took off like a rocket ship.

The good news was I was so busy that I decided to do this work full time. The bad news was I was severely conflicted between my sexual desire for several of these highly energetic, and in some cases extraordinarily attractive women, and my awareness that it was inappropriate to be having sex with a client. Fantasy and intrigue were running wild.

As time went by, the level of sexual seduction taking place between myself and some of these women was becoming more than I could manage. I decided to act on those impulses with many of these women after my work with them was complete. My rationalization was that this was appropriate and that the sex was *spiritual* or Tantric, empowering to both my partner and me.

It wasn't until I was confronted by one of my Chiron Brothers, at a time when I had crossed the line and was having sex with two of my current female clients, that I began to acknowledge I had a problem. I soon entered recovery for sexual addiction.

This began a four-year period of the deepest healing and transformation of my life, filled with lots of emotional pain. I got through those years, and now am enjoying a twelve plus year relationship with the only woman I've ever been faithful to.

In retrospect, it's my opinion that heterosexual men that are engaged in touch therapy with women should study ethics and boundaries through continuing education programs.

I would also recommend that these same men who choose this path, be under the supervision of a trained professional, the same as is required of psychotherapists. This supervision should continue as long as the therapist is practicing with female clients. I realize this may sound extreme, yet mine was an extreme case. Better to be safe than sorry.

Colin's Viewpoint

As you will notice when you read each person's reflections in the next section, especially their perceptions on each individual in the group, it was, and still is, their opinion that I was and am virtually non-sexual and have very little interest in sex.

As an emotional sexual, I would have appeared that way to a physical sexual, but it is not true. I just don't invest as much of my energy in it as physical sexuals do, or did then, at least.

They were also convinced that I did not share with them the same problem of sexuality arising between me as a healer and my clients. They were quite wrong. It was no less of an issue for me than it was for them, but I experienced it differently. But I think it was easier for me, I will say that.

As we saw in Chapter 2, emotionals process their sexual drives mainly through the mind and are very turned on by visual stimuli. Physicals are attracted to them because they seem to be, initially at least, impervious to their advances.

Emotionals do like the thrill of contemplating sexual activity so they are just as prone to falling prey to the seduction as the physicals if it should show up. They are also capable of having sex without being emotionally involved with the person whereas the physicals are more likely to become romantically hooked. So in that sense it was less of a problem for me emotionally.

That said, during the years I was single, I did cross the line a few times when I was doing hypnotherapy as a practice in the 80s and 90s. To be honest, I didn't worry about it at the time and didn't feel it was bad or wrong. Risky maybe, but not criminal. The women I had sex with were also single and were more than willing to play. I did not get emotionally involved with them though.

When I was teaching at Middlesex University, in the 70s, I also had some torrid affairs with a few of the mature students in my classes which, in hindsight now, could have gotten me into a lot of trouble. One of them was married, but I only discovered that while lying in bed basking in the afterglow. I was so shocked I dropped my cigarette and nearly set the bed on fire! I put an end to that very quickly, but this was the one woman who did latch on and became a bit of a problem.

I actually lived with one of my students for four years. We had agreed we would split after the fourth year because she was much younger than me and we both wanted different lives. That was hard, but it made sense. (Typical Emotional!)

It was really only when this topic came up in the group and saw how much of an issue it was for them that I gave a lot of consideration to the ethical question. I now see it as a real challenge for healers and an important issue that should be addressed very strongly in the training one does, providing clarity about the ethics of it and the harm it can do.

At first, I got a real kick out of hearing George talk about his sexual exploits and, frankly, I envied him. But, by that time I was married and, having committed to being monogamous,

I was not going to stray from that and never will. I had to be content with enjoying the stories and getting my excitement vicariously through him.

I also realized how lucky I had been in not ever having been reported, sued or beaten up by that one woman's husband. I am more than grateful.

To be honest, I don't regret any of it. I was careful and respectful of the women and I only had sex with them after therapy was complete.

People at that time didn't worry too much about such things. It is different today. Look at all the celebrities now being indicted for sexual assaults that happened years ago. Suddenly someone who in the past might have been referred to as 'a bit of a lad,' is now labelled a predator. If convicted, there is very little mercy shown. Be warned.

PART TWO

Personal Reflections on Being a Member of the Chiron Brotherhood from 1996 to the Present Day

NOTE: Please be aware that what follows is how each of us remembers 20 years' worth of meetings. That being the case, you may find them, to some extent at least, somewhat repetitive. Nevertheless, each person's recall of the events will vary since they were written separately, not collaboratively. That said, I hope you will find discovering the differences and the nuanced interpretation within each recounting of what took place, as well as what it meant for each of the men, interesting and evocative.

I should also say that the men have been very frank, honest and vulnerable in sharing their innermost feeling and revealing some parts of their lives they may not feel too proud of. Most of us have them, but few are willing to share them so openly. It takes courage.

My Reflections on Being Part of the Chiron Brotherhood

by George Poirier

In September 1994, after one of my workshops, Dennis and I decided to have dinner together. During dinner, Dennis mentioned that he and Greg had been to a men's movement workshop back in August in Greensboro, N.C. On the way home, they talked about the possibility of starting a men's group for male healers. Dennis and I thought it would be a great idea, and we developed the idea over dinner.

A week later, I called Dennis and asked him to have lunch with me at my apartment. Over lunch, we decided to initiate action and invite a group of male healers we knew and that we would like to be part of our group. I invited Farra, Tom, Rick, Colin and Gerry. Dennis invited Gregory.

One Saturday afternoon in October, Farra and I met Jack under synchronistic circumstance. We later invited Jack to join the group. Farra decided to invite Joe and Lou. Gerry extended an invitation to Wheel.

On November 18, 1994, the Chiron Brotherhood was born. We first met at Farra's home on Lake Lanier. Those who were in attendance that day included George, Farra, Gregory, Colin,

Dennis, Jack, Gerry, Joe, Wheel, and Lou. Lou and Wheel left on Saturday. Only Joe was destined to return.

The first thing we had to deal with was the logistics; how often we were to meet, and how we would come to decisions within the group. Almost immediately, power struggles arose among these very powerful egos. So the issues that we had to deal with almost from the beginning were ego issues within the group itself. I felt a lot of anxiety walking into this new group of men. There seemed to be an unspoken tension between Greg and me.

One of the things that we agreed on was to base all decisions on consensus. I believe that this decision was absolutely vital in keeping us all together, especially during our first year. The reason for this is that we battled, sometimes intensely, over every decision we made.

The first major battle that I had with Farra was over group attendance. I felt that if Joe came into the circle, he needed to stay for the entire weekend. He wanted to be able to come and go at any time he so pleased. This, usually, meant that Joe would stay for perhaps one day. We had agreed to meet Friday night to Sunday afternoon. Farra wanted to give Joe and everyone the flexibility to do that. I was adamant that everyone who came into the circle and created the synergy that had such a powerful healing effect needed to stay in that energy for the entire weekend. Farra and I battled over this time and time again; over several different weekends. This was a very rageful confrontation. Finally, we reached consensus, and Joe was told that if he were to attend our group meetings, he needed to stay for the entire weekend.

Confrontations over these issues were symbolic of the types of power issues that we dealt with on many levels for a good year.

The typical protocol that we employed was to begin our weekend with no agenda whatsoever. As these power issues would arise in the group, we would listen and confront each other in a way that was deeply penetrating. We'd employ various body centered techniques to process each of the brothers in a very deep level.

I had a lot of experience in various body/mind approaches for processing emotions that were being held in the body. Farra had founded a massage school and had done numerous trainings. I had been trained in Reichian bodywork. The other brothers have been trained in various healing techniques, and together we were a very effective and powerful force to enable us to support each other in processing through these various issues. But to say that these weekends were intense and transformational would be an understatement.

Amazingly, as intense and emotional as these weekends were, we all walked away feeling exhilarated and blessed. This was incredible, considering that at the time, we were all relative strangers. It took years to begin to understand how this was possible.

Greg and I began to discuss the past life possibilities of these relationships. Later, we all became aware of these implications.

News of this group and reports of the deep work being achieved began to spread within the healing community in the Atlanta area. We began to receive requests from several men wanting to join our group. At first, all were rejected. We knew we had something special, and we didn't want anything to upset the synergy of the group.

However, over time, we began to feel that we needed to share our experience with other men. Again, not all of us were in agreement on this issue. No surprise there. Particularly Farra, who was very much against the idea of bringing anybody else into the group. I and others in the group felt different, so we began to explore the possibilities of bringing in others. Again, Farra and I battled intensely over this.

Shortly thereafter, having again reached consensus, Phil and Michael became part of our circle.

I must say that during our initial time together, most of the issues that I experienced in the group, as far as my stuff being projected to my brothers, were a lot of unresolved anger issues that I had with my father from the time I was 3 years old. There was a fine line between being observant within the group, confronting other members in a loving way, and crossing that line in projecting anger and rage towards these guys. These other brothers were perceptive enough to watch me cross that line and then to confront me in ways that were almost unimaginable at the time. In retrospect, it's amazing that I would allow that type of confrontation to occur. What I was processing in the moment was intense fear and rage.

When it was my turn to get down on the mat and process, it took all six guys to hold me down. I was in a blind homicidal rage. This went on every 6 to 8 weeks for well over a year. And, I continued to process the same rageful feelings towards men, on and on and on.

One notable event took place in January, 1995. We happened to have a Chiron meeting at around the time of Farra's birthday. We decided to have a birthday party for him at the conclusion of our meeting, and we invited all of our wives, girlfriends and friends to the party. This was to begin immediately after we concluded our weekend together.

The shift in the energy that occurred when those other people walked into that house was unbelievable. This felt like in invasion to me. The crossing of some undeclared boundary. Women screaming with laughter. It just shattered the synergy of the group. We never did it again. Boundary issues were a recurring theme that Farra challenged us with over the years.

John joined the group in the early part of 1996.

A fun thing we did in 1996, around the time of Farra's birthday, was a sweat lodge on Lake Lanier. Gerry brought in a pipe carrier by the name of Philippe, who instructed us on how to build a sweat lodge ourselves. It was the best sweat lodge I have ever done. The energy was awesome and the experience was hilarious.

In the Spring of 1996, we attempted to take our process to other men as a group. We booked a group breathwork session for men only at the Marriott on I-85 North in Atlanta on a Saturday. The event was well attended. One attendee from Colorado injured Joe by tossing him across the room, and creating a hematoma on his knee. I invited Charlie, Larry, Randy and Jody as well as many others. It was quite a wild time. Typical male rage erupting all over the room. Lots of parallel processing occurred all day long.

As the group became more bonded, we began to share more of our sexual experiences. Saturday nights after dinner was when we would hang out and share our stories. I became the center of attention as we would talk freely about the women in our lives and the details of all the seduction and sex that was going on. I think the other brothers in the group were very much entertained, and were living their sexual lives vicariously through Farra and me. This became a regular event that everyone very much looked forward to.

During this time, we, as a group, confronted Gerry about his health. Mike and I felt strongly that Jerry's impending death was not that far away. This disturbed Gerry greatly. Shortly thereafter, Gerry left the group.

Later that year, Farra introduced the group to a book called *Radical Honesty.* Farra had done therapy with the author Brad Blanton in Washington DC years earlier. Around this time, our struggles began to peak, especially between Phil and Farra. Colin began to confront his fear of male power and dominance. Mike was his catalyst.

For the first time, Colin really got in all of our faces. It was great.

I decided to get a copy of the book, *Radical Honesty* and read it thoroughly. The philosophy of the book made sense to me, the essence of which was that to the degree to which we are able to be radically honest, especially around sexual relations with our partners, and emotionally with our close acquaintants, is the degree that we can truly transform.

The hypothesis was that lying, covering up, but not revealing our innermost demons was the cause of all psychological complexes. This really struck a chord within me, because I was being radically dishonest in my relationship with my wife.

The group began to discuss this philosophy on our weekends together. Farra was a big believer in the philosophy of this book, but the other brothers not so much. The more I read the book, the more I became interested in applying these concepts to my marriage. This scared the shit out of me.

Part of the process of the book was creating an intimacy checklist. The idea was that each partner would create such a list, and set aside a time where each person in the relationship would go through the list in great detail, revealing every secret fantasy and also sexual activities that took place from day one. Day one being, the start of one sexual life, all the way back to puberty.

My wife and I set a time to do this. I had quite a time putting my checklist together as I simply couldn't remember all of my sexual experiences from the time I was 15 years old. This included hundreds of experiences. However, I could remember 18 affairs that I had during the time of my marriage. As well as numerous fantasies and intrigue, which I revealed to my wife at the time.

When I later revealed this to the group, they were completely horrified. They couldn't believe that I had the balls to do this. I can't say they were happy about it. John especially was horrified by this. John felt that doing this, even by agreement, was a horrible projection, abuse and emotional dump on my wife. In retrospect, I believe John was right. But it was another year or so before I came to this conclusion.

This produced a radical shift in the group. Because now all the talk of sexual fun and games that would take place on Saturday night was no longer fun and games. The group began to shift its attention to relationships and sexuality. And instead of male power games, we began to confront each other on these issues. This produced great resistance within the group. A very different power struggle ensued.

In June, 1996, Phil invited me to lunch one day. Afterwards, we went over to Phil's apartment just to sit and talk. During the conversation, Phil confronted me, telling me that I was hiding behind radical honesty in order to have affairs with all these women. This included affairs that I had been having with two clients that Phil knew. Phil went on to say he felt like I had a severe sex addiction. I went into complete denial and began to project and confront Phil with the idea that he, in fact, was sexually interested in at least one of these women. Phil planted a seed in me that day that would later become a turning point in my life. He was the only brother in the group that had the balls to confront me in the way he did. Phil didn't pull any punches when he was confronting somebody. Ask Farra.

The confrontation that I had with Phil on that day struck deeply inside of me. At the time, I was sexually involved with two clients that I was seeing in my body/mind practice, and was making up all sorts of bullshit about spiritual sexuality. One evening, I woke up dreaming and began to journal all the feelings that I was experiencing during the dream.

The next morning, when I reviewed my journal, I realized that I was becoming psychotic and needed professional help. Phil had a lot of recovery experience. I called Phil and told him that I felt like I needed recovery help for this sexual addiction that he had confronted me with only a month before. He called me back and recommended a group that he thought was best suited to deal with my issues. I entered recovery for sexual addiction on August 15, 1996. This began a journey that changed my life forever in ways I couldn't even imagine.

It's difficult for me, even to this day, to really know how this experience in recovery really impacted all the brothers in the Chiron group. Part of the reason for this was that not all the men in this group were experiencing anything like the sexual issues that I was going through at the time. However, I wasn't sure whether or not some in the group were experiencing similar issues. Apparently, they were dealing with these issues in their own unique ways. These issues definitely changed the dynamics of the group. The recovery process for me was bringing up massive amounts of guilt and shame. These were mainly the issues that I was processing within the group as I was going through recovery.

65

Another member of the group was impacted by this, and decided to enter recovery himself. I'm not sure that the group felt that this was the ideal way to approach these issues for me. Yet, this was my path, and I don't regret it for one day. The reason for this is because after four grueling years of work and denial, I finally got to the point where I could see that my sexual addiction was separating me from my soul. At that point, I began to move into a state of wholeness and peace. In recovery terms, I began to realize the *promises*.

In October, 1996, Farra, George, Phil and Jack enrolled in an NLP Practitioner training with Peggy D. This event was to have a huge impact on our group. Over the years, the two guys in the group that I had developed a close personal relationship with outside of the group were Jack and Farra.

Jack and I had actually started working together doing a process that we called *Breakthrough* at his home on Lake Lanier. Jack and I had also started doing a lot of processing together, just the two of us, during the summer months of the same year. Jack was the first to meet Peggy D., and brought the idea of us doing the NLP training together at one of our Chiron meetings. The initial deal that he negotiated was four of us would do the training for the price of three. However, on the first weekend when we actually got to the training, we were told by Peggy's trainer that the discount was to be given to Jeanne. I was furious and confronted the trainer, threatening to leave along with Farra and Phil if we didn't all get the discount. The trainer decided to be reasonable about it and he gave us the discount. On a boat ride with him one day on Lake Lanier, I confronted Jack with how it was that this happened.

For reasons that I still don't understand, Jack and I never resolved this issue. It's my belief that whatever was going on deep within Jack at the time, as well as all that was triggered during the NLP training subconsciously led to Jack's withdrawal from the training and, ultimately, the group about a month later.

In December, 1996, we had a Chiron meeting at Farra's house in Virginia Highlands. I believe that Farra, Phil, Jack, Colin and I were present. Friday nights were when everybody got to the designated place of our meetings.

On the weekend we arrived, Farra decided to entertain a beautiful young woman from California. We were all a little shocked that this was occurring. This was no joke to us, as this broke a clear agreement that we had within the group not to include women in any part of the process or gathering.

Jack was the least amused among the group. So much so, that the following day, Jack announced that he was leaving the group. The reason he stated was that we were continuously dealing with repetitive issues around sexuality and relationships and not moving through them. This caused one of the most severe eruptions in the group that I can ever recall. Farra starting throwing plastic bottles of water around the room, glass was breaking, furniture was moving around, and amazingly, Phil fell fast asleep in a rocking chair. Farra started shaking Phil and screaming, "Wake up you motherfucker."

I was completely blown away by what Jack was telling us. He was one of the most committed guys in the group. Up until that time, he was one of the few of us that had never missed a Chiron meeting. I was angry and depressed, felt totally abandoned by Jack, and stayed that way for a good month. This was definitely one of our darkest hours together. Jack's story is that he needed to move on, I felt like that was total bullshit. My codependent issues were raging. In the end, I just had to let him go.

During the last quarter of 1996 and as the NLP training was progressing, I decided to offer Colin an opportunity to work with me five days a week. He was hitting an emotional bottom at the time, and I wanted to help him to the best of my ability. We did this work together for about a month, and at the end of that month, Colin announced to me that he was going to take time off and write a book on Radical Forgiveness. I have to say that Colin's ability to transmute this work successfully into his writing and teaching career has been just wonderful for all of us to observe. We're all very proud of him.

A month later, in January 1997, we decided to have a week-end with the wives at a beautiful estate on the Chattahoochee River. We invited Jack and Dennis, who showed up with their wives. It was a cool weekend just hanging out, and doing some light processing work. Nothing too heavy or intense. And that's the last we saw of Jack and Dennis for a very long time. In fact, I don't think I talked to Jack for another 10 years.

Sometime in March 1997, the remaining members of the group decided to create a Mastermind group. We would con-vene through a conference call at a predetermined time on a particular weekday.

It was during this time that the original members of the group, especially me, came to the conclusion that the original decision to expand the membership of the group beyond the original members was a mistake. We concluded and made a very painful decision to remove Phil and Mike from the group.

As tough as this was for me, I have to admit that Farra was right from the beginning on this issue and that this was all for the good. It was at this time that it became apparent that there was strong karmic past life connections among these original members.

In April of the same year, we decided to have a couple's weekend when we would open up with the wives in the same fashion as we had within the group. Colin thought we were completely out of our minds, for we were in no way as honest with our spouses as we were with each other. He predicted a total disaster and declined to participate in this debacle.

Colin could not have been righter about anything. That was the weekend that I very nearly left the group. On Saturday of that weekend, my wife began to interrogate both Farra and Gregory on issues that she felt we were processing within our group that she was unaware of. During that interrogation, Gregory began to share with her details that I had processed previously within the group and that I had not revealed to her concerning certain feelings that I had about the relationship. I could not believe what I was listening to. Feeling totally betrayed by Greg and infuriated, I damn near left the group on the spot. For me, this was a deep violation of the trust that we had slowly and painfully built up over the years within the group.

Luckily, Gregory and I were able to resolve the issue within the context of the group. It always amazes me when I recall these incidents, how we managed to stay together all these years. In July of 1997, my wife and I ended the marriage.

In October, 1997 I was living in Morningside and decided to have the Chiron meeting at my place. The group decided again to invite male guests to our meeting. Colin extended an invitation to Ross and Reggie. I invited Mark, Jody and Charlie. This may have been one of the more successful efforts of sharing our process with other men, yet I'm not sure that the other brothers would agree.

In March of the following year, I moved in with Farra, then the group began to meet regularly at our home in Virginia Highlands. The focus on sexuality and relationship issues began to intensify as Farra and I effectively turned our house into a giant fraternity party.

In 1998 to 2000, I was really struggling with sex addiction issues both in recovery and within the context of our group. This work paid big dividends in the future. At the time, it felt like a continuous struggle. I can't thank my brothers enough for hanging in there with me. This includes my brothers in recovery and the Chiron group.

In September, 1998, Gerry succumbed to a heart attack. We held a memorial at his widow's apartment, where she promptly hit on Colin! Apparently she couldn't get enough of those Chiron Brothers.

In my opinion, one of the most fun things that we did one evening, as a group, was organizing a group breathwork session with students at the University of Georgia. Moses and James organized this for us, and it was held at an old church in Athens, Georgia. The church was packed with between 50 and 60 kids. I had never done this work with young people before, and had no idea what kind of reaction we'd get from them.

Their reaction was overwhelming. We combined breathwork with evocative music and movement. And these kids went apeshit. That was so cool! They just loved it. This was sort of a reprieve from all the really heavy adult type processing that would normally happen anytime we got together. These kids knew how to make our work fun.

Sometime in early 2000, Sam decided to crash one of our meetings. Sam was part of a group that was formed at the Aware House who were into systems and chaos theories, as they played out in organizations. Sam was really an interesting guy. He confronted me as intensely as anybody did about what he called my *gig*. Sam was all about pointing out how people unconsciously created reality, and almost immediately projected and denied it. Sam was relatively mild the day he visited the group and, although uninvited, he was well-received.

Later that spring, I'd had been having an affair with a gal that suddenly became psychotic and sent letters to Colin, Farra, the woman I was dating at the time and me. In the letter, she was going on about what a terrible person I was. Who, me?

I got to the point where I was over dealing with all the projection and decided that I didn't want to see her in our house anymore. Unfortunately, she lived in the neighborhood and would crash our place without notice. Farra had befriended her and had become an advocate. So now Farra and I were clashing over her unannounced presence in our home.

This became a deal breaker for me. Not so much for him. I took the issue to the Chiron group, and, lucky for us, Colin saved the day. He listened to both sides of our conflict and turned to Farra and said, "Are you prepared to lose your brother over this?" Farra's response was, "No." This was sort of the beginning of the end for me living with Farra in Virginia Highlands.

The last Chiron meeting during, what I call the formative years from 94 to 2000, occurred in the summer of 2000 at Farra's house. I was beginning to work with Dennis in Highlands, North Carolina, and on January 25, 2001 moved to there permanently. At this last meeting, I gave my Star of David medallion to Greg. It was quite a piece, made of optically clear quartz crystal, and cut in a three-dimensional Star of David in the center of an equilateral triangle. The medallion represented to me the culmination of all the work we accomplished together. Not knowing if we would ever reconvene, I was symbolically passing the mantle to Greg to continue the work.

This was followed by a seven-year sabbatical for the brotherhood. During this time, I had little to no contact with any of my brothers, except for Farra and Greg.

On April 14, 2007, Phil succumbed to a heart attack one day after I had done a Reichian session with him at his apartment. I received a phone call from his daughter announcing his death. My whole body went numb. I had just seen him the previous day. Jack represented us at his funeral.

I subsequently called Jack, having not talked to him for over 10 years. It felt as natural with Jack on the telephone that day as it always had. I suggested to Jack that we reconvene the group. Jack was all for it. So, in August, 2007, the Chiron Brothers reconvened after a seven-year sabbatical. Jack, Greg, Dennis, Colin, Farra, Joe and I were all present. Joe attended one or two more weekends with us. Dennis never returned.

In February, 2008, during one of our meetings, the group decided to take psychedelic mushrooms and I sat for the group, refraining from taking any so I could assist anyone who might have a problem or any issues that arose. We repeated this again in August. I again sat with the group. We integrated the sessions with artwork and movement.

In August, 2013, Jack, Farra and I did Reichian bodywork again for the first time since the 90s. It was great. I got to process the death of my infant brother back when I was three years old. Jack was amazing that day.

A word about Dennis. He may have been the most enigmatic member of the group. He was absolutely instrumental in the initiation of our group. Dennis and I have a close, heart-centered connection. I lived with Dennis for a year and a half, and worked with him for seven years.

Dennis really struggled with the massive egos within the group. He was with us less than two years and missed many of our gatherings during that time period. If it hadn't been for the lady he was living with at the time encouraging him to attend, he may have withdrawn earlier. Dennis was terrified to be confronted by these very strong men. I must admit, I had a soft spot in my heart for Dennis. I protected him, especially from Farra, made excuses for his nonparticipation.

Paradoxically, I was determined to confront everyone else in the group. I was definitely the *take no prisoners* guy in the group. But with Dennis, my perception was that he was one of these personalities that would not, or could not tolerate intense introspection without suffering a psychotic break. I was very much in touch with Dennis's sensitivity.

Farra, on the other hand, really confronted Dennis's fears and did so rigorously. Dennis would start to crumble right before our eyes. This was especially true one weekend at Greg's in Boone. It got so bad that Dennis was going to leave the group on a Saturday afternoon. I intervened and confronted Farra about pushing him too far. At that point, Farra wanted Dennis out of the group. I guess in the end he got his wish.

That was the end for Dennis. I was very confused and sad about the loss of Dennis, yet I had to accept the fact that he never really got integrated into the group. That being said, the group failed to create safe containment for Dennis to process and integrate his intense feelings. Dennis and I still maintain a very close relationship. I will always miss his presence in the group.

Compiler's Note:

When we discussed what to include in the book, we thought it would be revealing if we included, in each of our reflections, our impressions of each other. With the exception of George and Farra, who lived together for a couple of years, we hardly socialized at all between group meetings, and yet we came to know each other pretty well. Here are George's impressions of the five remaining members.

My Perception of My Chiron Brothers:

Colin:

I first met Colin in October, 1993. He attended one of the workshops I was conducting in Atlanta, Georgia. My first impressions of Colin was that he seemed to be a somewhat sophisticated Brit, rather shy and sort of a quiet guy. He was articulate and a great communicator.

When we first started the Chiron group he seemed to be a bit nervous and timid around these big egos. It later became clear that he was holding back and wasn't accessing his full power within the group. It was obvious that he was creative. He loved teaching and was very adept at putting together programs and presentations. At first, he seemed to be more tolerant towards the other brothers and more compassionate and empathetic.

As I got to know Colin over a period of years, I realized what a taskmaster he was, and is, towards himself and others. When he takes on a project, he really likes to ring it out and see it through to the very end. I definitely see Colin as the archetype of the teacher. He is the most cautious and guarded member of the group.

What I admire the most about Colin is his ability to accept and not judge people because of some personal defect or shortcoming. Colin naturally accepts people with their imperfections. He has a remarkable ability to do this, and not lose his sense of discernment.

The paradoxical and enigmatic part of him is that while he lands in the world as tolerant and compassionate, in his personal life I've seen him erupt and unleash furious and demeaning anger at those who love and admire him the most.

Colin probably demonstrates the most profound change and transformation of all the brothers. This is especially true in going from being timid and fearful of powerful men, as well as his own power, to fully embracing his potential and transmuting it into all of his creative projects. His story is literally rags to riches.

What I've learned from this brother is tenacity, determination and perseverance in pursuing one's dream. Even in the face of destitution, he kept reaching for whatever resources would empower him to achieve his goal of bringing Radical Forgiveness to the world. He's been an inspiration to us all.

Greg:
Greg is the most driven member of the group, landing as a powerful extrovert. He lights up a room when he walks in. Greg is a very effective communicator, extremely ambitious and energetic. He's always got to be doing something. He can't stand to just sit and do nothing. He can be a bit stubborn at times, but this is part of what gives him his drive.

At times, Greg can project impatience and a judgmental attitude. He is a very passionate person, loves his freedom and is willing to take risks. He may be a bit too survival oriented at times, but that's the way it is.

Greg may be the most intuitive and insightful brother in the group. Trust comes slow and hard for him. He is the intuitive archetype.

I really admire Greg's intuition and insight. He sees deeply into situations. Greg and I often agree on what we see going on behind the veil. Also, his skill at delineating how spirit is directing and guiding us is remarkable.

The major change I've observed in Greg is the healing that's taken place with his ex-wife and children. 20 years ago, Greg was suffering mightily with these issues. Today, he greatly enjoys his interactions with his family. Also, his practice has grown from a local practice in Atlanta to a successful international practice that takes him around the world.

The enigmatic part of Greg is his sexuality. He's a very sexual guy and I'm sure has had many opportunities to experience lots of women in his travels. Yet, he's suppressed these impulses. I've always felt that Greg is intensely conflicted with this dynamic in his life. He acted in. I acted out.

What I've learned from Greg is to stay the course. I have a propensity to jump from one interest to another, which tends to scatter my energy. Greg has taught me the value of not deviating from my intention. Once I begin to move on a chosen path, to stay on that path. Greg has been most skillful at supporting and guiding me to continue on my current path as an empowered mentor for others. He, more than the others, has been sensitive to the lengthy integration period I've been going through in recent years. He continues to lovingly nudge me along with his love and support.

Farra:

Farra epitomizes the *Puer Aeternus* (eternal youth) archetype of the group. He has enormous charisma, which is his winning formula, and is the mask he uses to hide his not enoughness. You can always hear the volume of his voice above the others. He's the cool dude of the group. Loves to party and have fun. Farra will endeavor to make fun out of everything he does. Life of the party type guy.

Farra just loves the type of body/mind processing we do in this group. More is better. Very impulsive. We first met over lunch at Dennis's one day, and when he heard about the work I did, he wanted a session with me on the spot.

Farra is passionate about life and will NEVER give up on his dream or anyone he loves.

The boy has definite boundary issues that we've battled for 20 years. He is always attempting to alter plans. Farra is a great coach and motivator.

What I admire and enjoy most about Farra are the enthusiasm and excitement he brings to all aspects of his life. Farra is also, the most wonderful friend to have. He's very magnetic. He's always there to champion me and my efforts with encouragement and love.

The enigmatic part of Farra is his repetitive propensity to violate boundaries and agreements without hesitation or awareness. It seems he will, usually, try to alter agreed plans. This is perplexing considering all the EST training that he'd participated in over the years in which keeping agreements was a central tenet of the work. Nevertheless, this enigma continues to this day. I believe this to be a result of his Gemini Moon. This also comes from a deep neediness that's a result of his repressed unworthiness.

The biggest change in Farra over the last 20 years has been in his woundedness and desperation. He no longer is constantly seeking a new identity or looking for someone to lean on to accomplish his goals. He has discovered the abundant resources within himself to actualize his mission of empowering others in being all that they can be.

What I've learned from Farra, is once one has discovered their purpose and passion, they must pursue it with great vigor. Or, in other words, never give up on one's dream or those that they love.

Jack:

Jack is an intelligent, strong personality, highly analytical and no nonsense. He is a serious dude. He is a show me the results type guy, not an esoteric type. Whatever Jack is up to must make sense. A man of reason. Where are we going, are we making progress? These questions are important to Jack. He is very pragmatic.

He projects a certain rigidness and lack of flexibility. At times, he can be a bit prickly and impatient.

Jack has a strong sense of commitment to a particular project, but it must make sense. He expects the same level of commitment in return. This, as much as anything, I believe, attracted Jack to this group. Male abandonment is huge for him. Jack is very loyal. Trust is everything for Jack; "Are you going to be there on the rope with me?"

Jack's ability with focused intent is beyond anything I've ever witnessed. Jack is the goal-oriented achiever archetype of the group.

What I admire most about Jack is his groundedness. His ability to focus his intent and direct his actions in the most efficient and pragmatic way to achieve his goal.

The enigmatic part is his tendency to annihilate anything in his life that he deems unresourceful. It's like it never existed. There is an internal mechanism triggering this that baffles me.

The changes in Jack in the last 20 years is that he's much more comfortable in his own skin and in the presence of the group. Much more present and not as tightly wound. Today, Jack is just as content to letting this happen as he is with making them happen.

What I've learned from Jack is balance in all areas of life. Jack will not be pulled into extremes like me, or like I did in the past. If he sees me being pulled into an extreme, he's there to move me back into balance, usually with bodywork or just a few words. Jack is a wonderful, loving support for me.

Finally, I would like to say that my years, especially the first six years, in the Chiron Brotherhood, were clearly the most transformational years of my life. It was absolutely an amazing experience for me. I'll always feel gratitude and appreciation for the courage that it took for my brothers to be present and supportive with their gifts in my life. My hope is that sharing these experiences will encourage others to confront their shadow issues with courage.

My Reflections on Being Part of the Chiron Brotherhood

by Rev. Dr. Gregory Possman

Terror, suspicion, a sense of inadequacy and anxiety were the feelings with which I entered my first moment in the Chiron Brotherhood.

My reactions and relations to men prior to beginning this work had always been feelings of distrust, competition, and the feeling of uneasiness in terms of getting closer to men. If I ever bonded with a male figure in my life, it was, usually, as a friend.

Although those friendships lasted for a few years, they never lasted for a lifetime. It was always my nature to move from place to place. If I were not the one moving, then the one I'd befriended would move.

This was my excuse for terminating long-lasting relationships with male friends. As I reflect on my pattern, I realize very little trust was ever established due to the short nature of these relationships. It was my belief that these hurdles in my life could be addressed, and perhaps overcome, by my involvement in the Chiron Brotherhood.

While growing up I remember my father, Jack Richard Possman, always working one full-time job, and one or more part-time jobs. Although, in retrospect, he did more activities and spent more time with my brother, sister and me than I wanted to give him credit for. At the same time, he did work quite a lot. My recollection was spending many nights and weekends wondering when my father would be arriving home. To my father's credit, I inherited his ambition, his drive and his motivation. Success was always important to me.

I began my Chiron experience, comparing myself to the other men in the group. Our first day, as I remember it, was a giant testosterone test. We were all jockeying for position, in terms of dictating rules the group would observe in its future. The power struggles were immense. I also remember tallying up in my head the differences, judgments and criticisms of the other men in the group.

The first weekend left me wondering if I would ever return. However, I knew that in order to conquer my issues with trust, I would have to return.

Commitment to the group, or the lack of it, was a huge factor in terms of the group's largest issue. It felt as though no one was willing to commit to attending more of the gatherings, which were a weekend in duration, unless everyone made it a priority. It was clear that abandonment by men was a huge issue. I know that I would not have returned if I thought the other men in the group did not hold the process as important as I did.

Specifically, I remember the similarities I had with some of the men in the group. I could immediately relate to George Poirier as he and I had many common experiences and traits. We had both come from successful business careers. We both met our current partners after we had become healers. We had children from previous relationships and we shared a common intuitive ability, which at the time, I could not really define.

Our conversations helped me to confirm my own confidence in my work as a psychic trance channel, which is of a highly spiritual and intuitive nature. The most powerful similarity was a complete conversion from left-brained activity to a right-brained type of work. These commonalities helped me to feel as if I had an ally in the group. Had I not made that connection, it's hard to say whether I would have continued to participate.

I was also immediately taken with Farra Allen. He seemed larger-than-life and his enthusiasm was magnetic. I remember first meeting Farra at a large house that he rented on Lake Lanier, near Gainesville, Georgia. I was invited to a party there. On the roof, there were people drumming and the roof started making noises, at which point, it seemed as though the roof was collapsing. Someone yelled, "Everyone off!" and people quickly descended to the ground.

At that time, Farra appeared to me to be a veritable party animal. Farra Allen is truly larger-than-life. The first thing that struck me about Farra was his name. It's a name I had never heard before, and I questioned or wondered where it came from. After 20 years of knowing this brother, I've been told by Farra that his namesake was his Grandfather. To this day he is the only person I know named Farra. Farra always seems to be searching for something more, there being a deeper meaning, a different experience, or a new height to attain. Farra has calmed down in the last 20 years and has become loyal to one partner. This represents to me a deeper love for self. Having given himself the gift of a loyal partner.

I'm happy to say that I've gotten to know Farra very well. Farra had been very successful in his business activities and there was no reason to believe that would change. Farra, who started the Atlanta School of Massage, was eventually bought out by his ex-wife, Leticia. It was obvious the buy-out created a huge hole in Farra's identity. Farra dug and dug into every possible mysterious meaning of his past. He would analyze those meanings to no end. Letting go of the past was extremely difficult for him.

Those are the facts as I saw them and Farra is a very complex man. He appears on the surface to be very enthusiastic, nonconformist, and grandiose. He has an infectious smile, while inside he is very sensitive, fragile, and anxious. I have learned to take better care of myself from Farra's example. I have also learned to show more enthusiasm for life and love for others, as at times, I can be seen as very aloof.

I took a liking to all of the men in the group; however, I remember being most impressed by Farra and George Poirier. George and I had met earlier on a Universal Brotherhood cruise to the Bahamas. I remember being impressed with the beauty of George's wife, Kathleen. Beautiful women seldom ever missed my attention.

I had heard about George from a mutual friend of ours, who had sponsored his work in Atlanta, where I was living at the time. I remember sitting in a hot tub, sometime during our Brotherhood experience, conversing with George. I was struck with how similar we were in terms of our work, our lives and our personalities. I could relate to his stories of success in work as well as his feelings about his family and his siblings.

I was also struck by the similarities of our spiritual paths, both of us having come from very left-brained, sales oriented, successful businesses. We shared a similar introduction to the spiritual realms and the process of making it our lifework. We had so much in common, it seemed as though there would be a great deal for us to explore. George's certainty and confidence impressed me.

Though I always strove for that appearance of confidence and knowingness, I never truly felt I had it inside. My sense of insecurity could be hidden from others; however, George did not seem to have that characteristic. He knew who he was, what he was doing and his direction.

George struck a nerve in me when he told me about being estranged from his two sons. Having left my ex-wife and three children, this upset me. I remember encouraging George to reconnect with his sons. My ex-wife had moved back to her family in Miami. Since I was living in Atlanta, Georgia, I was triggered by George's lack of participation in his son's lives. In retrospect, and knowing more now than I did then, it was none of my business. I was simply projecting my own feelings of guilt and abandonment on George as I had left my first wife and children.

George's curiosity and desire to learn are what I admire most about him. Although George has tremendous gifts and can be of great service to people, he prefers the lifestyle of the hermit. I've always felt he could help so many people, and at one point in his life, he did. Now he prefers his peace, privacy and quiet, using this time to research and read using his iPad.

George has found inner peace within himself and no longer indulges in sexual encounters with multiple partners. He has created a long-term relationship and is loyal to his partner. He has also become more sure of himself than he was before. I also see an increase in his dedication to his family. I have learned from George to forge ahead with courage and force. I have also learned to disregard many of my fears in the process. George has taught me that great change is not only possible, it is imminent.

On the first weekend of the Brotherhood, I grew tired of the bickering over the rules. I felt we had more important issues to discuss than when we would meet again and what the excusable reasons for absence would be.

I felt an immediate connection to another time or place, where we had done this before. I could not identify when or where, yet I knew this was not our first rodeo. I sensed we had failed in that previous gathering together. Knights of the Templar, the Masons, and thoughts around protection, initiation, and even some sort of spiritual awakening ran through my mind.

I wasn't very confident at the time, and, therefore, kept most of these thoughts to myself. Though I could have channeled beings from the other side at our gatherings, I hesitated to do so. That would've been more exposure than I was comfortable with.

Despite the fear and misgivings about trusting these men, a sense of camaraderie, brotherhood and fellowship started almost immediately. It was one of the greatest dualities I had ever experienced. Although I was often nervous about what I was to do or say next, I realized the atmosphere of these gatherings would become safer and safer.

I also realized these gatherings would become more important to me. I had always had premonitions of the future and feelings about my activities. The Chiron Brotherhood would have some great purpose in my life though I didn't know what it was. I had no idea how strong and influential my participation in the group would be for me.

Whenever a heated discussion took place, and initially there were many, I remember wanting to leave the room. My fear of conflict and violence was difficult to overcome. The fight or flight reaction within me, often stared me in the face. For some reason, I was rooted to that room.

There seemed to be an unwritten rule that violence was unacceptable. The rage and anger I saw expressed by men, triggered by one another in that group, was fierce. Countless times, it seemed as though fisticuffs were about to occur, but never did. Although there were physical expressions of rage and anger when we were doing body/mind work, to my recollection, there were no actual fist fights. Having the different healers present in the room made for an experience of multiple therapies, forms of methodology and healing, which led to incredible processing. It was as if magic were taking place.

Though I had never experienced psychiatric or psychological therapy, I often remember thinking how quickly and rapidly we moved through our issues, based on varying points of view, offered by all of these healers simultaneously. Insight, observations, and methods of moving through seemed to pop out of the woodwork. The differing experiences, personalities and training present was incredibly effective in working through suppressed and repressed emotions. Immediately, issues cropped up for most of us while the processing that ensued, usually, triggered another man into his own process.

The imbalance of masculine and feminine energy was one of these themes. Sexuality and how each of us approached it was also a very large topic of discussion. Farra Allen's drug use combined with my imagination about his sexual antics were stories that fascinated me. Since I grew up as a very well-behaved young man, seeming to have missed the free love and drug culture, Farra's stories were always welcome. Farra never ran out of experiences, lucid dreams, descriptions of wild sexual encounters and captivating stories about women he had met. I remember wondering if any human being could really have had all of those experiences. Certainly I had not.

Accepting our own God/Goddess feminine self was another aspect we touched on frequently. Like Farra, George Poirier began relaying his sexual experiences to me. I was critical of his sexual relationships with female clients. Having been warned against this behavior and the possibility of it early in my spiritual career, I encouraged George to stop these relationships. The more I warned against it, the more he seemed to escalate. I realized we had had some kind of past life experience together, and I felt as though I needed to protect him.

90

Although I wanted more details about that life, I didn't get them. I had an overwhelming sense of future disaster as a result of George's sexual encounters with his clients. He even recommended some of those clients to me.

On occasion, I was jealous. However, due to my own colored past, I never made any advances on these women. Over the years, I lived vicariously through George's experiences. I was jealous of all the experiences he had, and I never tired of listening to his recounting of them. I knew the axe would fall one day and projected all my own fears on him. This only seemed to increase George's bravado and careless lack of concern for the consequences of his actions. Although it frightened me, secretly, I admired that bravado.

In the Brotherhood, expression of our rage, anger, shame, guilt, and fear became commonplace. We realized very quickly that perhaps we had finally found a safe place to express these emotions. The words *real deal* constantly arose when referring to the work.

Contrary to popular opinion, there was minimal complaining about female mates, wives or girlfriends. Though I'm certain the occasional complaint was registered, we focused primarily on our own issues and utilized the time to heal. We quickly realized how valuable this time together was. I had never experienced a place where losing control of my emotions was not only considered acceptable, but encouraged.

I had elbows ground into my solar plexus; I was physically restrained while screaming, raging, and crying, and grew more familiar with feeling an incredible release and catharsis afterward. This became commonplace and very therapeutic.

91

We often commented that if we were to videotape these sessions, they would probably sell very quickly. We also speculated that women, had they been flies on the wall, would probably find our gatherings very different than they would have expected. I had no idea how many demons, dark energies and black feelings were commonplace amongst men. Nor did I have any idea how many such feelings were pent-up inside of me. I felt that if all men had the opportunity to partake of this group, the nation's prisons would be emptied in a short period of time.

I often sensed the presence of light beings around us. Usually, these beings were benevolent and kind. On occasion, however, I felt the presence of something menacing. We began using sage, prayers, and other tools such as crystals to cleanse ourselves after the work was done. A swim in the lake, a soak in the hot tub or just peaceful conversation with a male companion were often soothing and healing experiences after an intense day of processing.

The greatest experience of community occurred for me when our group decided to build and experience our own sweat lodge. Someone arranged for a water pourer to join us on a Saturday. In the morning, we began building the lodge, based upon instructions we had intuited, since the water pourer who was to instruct us was delayed. Although it took time, the lodge seemed to come together with amazing speed. I witnessed and experienced a powerful sense of cooperation, and a sense of service.

During the lodge, we were encouraged to pray, sing, contemplate and release. The feeling of companionship and grace was overwhelming for me. I had seldom experienced such a communal, spiritual event in my life.

I have had the opportunity to be baptized at Lourdes in France, where the Mother Mary had appeared to a number of observers. The water at Lourdes was very cold and I remember feeling it was a miracle that it practically dried on my body in seconds. That baptism, though I am not Catholic, nor religious, was also an intense experience.

The experience in the sweat lodge with my Chiron Brothers was equally impactful. It felt as if the Creator had joined us in that sweat lodge. I remember after, walking down to Lake Lanier. I had every intention of swimming in the lake. As I stood on the pier, I felt a pressure against my chest. There was nothing visible in front of me. This invisible force on my chest pushed me backward toward the shore. Had I not shuffled my feet underneath me in a backward direction, I would have fallen backward.

It was obvious that something did not want me to swim on that day. It was clearly protection of some kind, designed for my well-being. I gathered my towel and headed back toward the lodge.

That day is etched in my memory forever. I will never forget the sense of community and brotherhood I experienced. Nor will I forget the power of that force that kept me out of the water. I am forever grateful to the Creator, the water pourer, Philippe and to my Chiron brothers who participated in the sweat lodge for that experience.

At some point in the evolution of our process, we decided the energy of the group would rise and the work would become deeper if certain members were no longer a part of our group. We consciously decided that those who were not committed to their growth should leave.

Growing up as the oldest child in a family of five, I realized I had become a flaming co-dependent. When these conversations took place regarding forcing a member to leave, overwhelming uneasiness always occurred within me. I usually wanted to speak in the member's defense, encouraging the group not to *fire* the individual. In retrospect, asking them to leave was the most appropriate action. It always seemed as if the energy rose, once the specific member had terminated his participation in our group.

The outcome was always a more intense level of safety, trust and a willingness to work at a deeper level. Usually, the one asked to leave was unwilling to face his issues with authenticity and a sincere desire to change. It felt as though these men were dancing around the truth. I respect these men, for having participated in the brotherhood for as long as they did. I miss them, as I have little or no contact with them anymore.

Several have passed away and it seems as though their spirits and their souls are still with us. Although he left of his own accord, Dennis McCauley was one of these men. I would describe Dennis as a dreamer and a man who always encouraged the best from the universe. Dennis and John Lennon could have been Brothers. Usually, Dennis was quiet and reserved. Parts of Dennis are childlike in a way. He had difficulty accepting the world as it was. He always wanted the most optimistic possible view of everything. Definitely a seeker, Dennis never tired of looking deeper and deeper into something to determine its spiritual value. Dennis could see deeply into many things, even those things he didn't accept and didn't like.

Dennis always took his time, moved slowly and was very deliberate in everything he did. I never had the patience Dennis required. I always wanted to move more quickly and found it difficult to wait for him. I couldn't take the time to smell the coffee, or roses, or whatever someone is supposed to smell when they slow down.

A deep thinker, Dennis is also a researcher, spending a great deal of time on the Internet and sharing whatever he finds that he feels will benefit his friends and family.

A great massage therapist, Dennis can always calm someone down. Given his retirement, I imagine Dennis has all the time he needs now to do whatever his spirit guides him to do.
We often remember the men who have left willingly, or otherwise, in our opening or closing circle. We include the spirits of the men who have passed away. We often talk about their contributions to our group and the role they played in the process. There is no regret for having let them go. We speak of them with honor and respect. A conscious decision to keep the energy level of the group as high as possible has paid off.

A decision to use consensus rather than majority rule also paid off. The concept means that if any man disagrees with a particular policy or activity, his wishes were honored and that concept or activity would be vetoed. It didn't matter if only one man in the group disagreed, his opinion was seen as the universe's way of expressing the truth to us. The same policy is used amongst other organizations.

I have little knowledge of whom, however, amongst elders, councils and other organizing contingents, it appears that this form of decision-making has been working for a very long time. Learning to honor our intuition has been a difficult lesson.

Another tough decision involved deciding when the group would be closed to new members. On several occasions, someone wanted to add a friend or acquaintance to the group, arguing that this individual had so much to offer. I remember wanting to invite a friend of mine into the group. Overwhelming objection was the result. No one but I knew this man. Therefore, no one wanted to admit him into our group. The other group members did not want to expend the energy necessary to begin establishing trust all over again. My friend's admittance to the group would have changed the energy and the chemistry.

Once again, the wisdom of consensus was proven. It had nothing to do with the personality of the individual. It had only to do with the process which would have to begin again if a new member were added. One can argue that greater contributions to the group could be made by new members; however, the re-establishing of trust is too high a price to pay.

Another peak experience for me in the Chiron Brotherhood occurred when we were meeting in Atlanta, Georgia, specifically in Virginia Highlands, at the next home of Farra Allen. It seemed that, as usual, synchronicity had occurred at a very deep level. We had been discussing an individual, a friend of George Poirier. Interestingly enough, this man made an appearance at Farra's home while we were meeting. To my knowledge he had not been invited. We concurred that this was the Universe giving us what we needed and we invited him in. He imparted some insight to each of us and then departed as quickly as he had shown up.

Later in the day we were sitting around Farra's dining room table enjoying a meal. It was summer and the front door was open since it was quite warm. A huge white dog, a Great Pyrenees, walked in through the front door and walked around the dining room table greeting each of us. The dog acted as if he were in his own home and had no resistance to any of us. He was calm and peaceful. He allowed each of us to pet him and eventually his owner came through the front door, commenting that the dog had never done this before. The owner apologized to which we replied that no apology was necessary. The dog had added a great deal to our experience. The dog and the owner left as we all smiled to one another, understanding that this was another perfect synchronicity in our process.

Even though I grew up in the drug culture of the 1960s and 1970s, I never experienced it. The Brotherhood provided me with the opportunity to experience the altered consciousness of Psilocybin Mushrooms. The Brothers had decided to try mushrooms together at one of our weekend gatherings. It was also decided that we would experience this in ritual form.

One of our members, George Poirier, would remain conscious and refrain from taking the mushrooms, in order to support those having the experience. I did not eat breakfast that morning as I was aware of the effects these mushrooms have on the stomach, primarily that of vomiting. We had all smudged ourselves and been quiet for a few moments as we passed the mushrooms around. I ate four of them.

About thirty minutes later I began to hallucinate. I had visions of our group going through various initiations, being tattooed, tortured, and performing some service together which I could not see clearly. Eventually, I decided to sit at the base of the large tree in Jack Winner's backyard (also on Lake Lanier) where we had begun meeting. As I sat at the base of the tree, I could see ants walk toward me in a line. I imagined that they were going to sting me if I stayed at the base of the tree.

It seemed very important that I go out toward the lake to escape the ants. Making it to the shore seemed like a battle, in my less than conscious state. In my altered state of consciousness, it was a very difficult process to achieve physically. Relieved to have reached the water, I entered the lake and I felt as if I had escaped the ants, which I knew were symbolic of some much greater adversary.

Having fully immersed myself in the water, I returned to the house and to the upper deck where I sat down on a stool and leaned over the rail. Overlooking the backyard and the lake, I began to feel immense waves of grief. I cried and cried, not only about the experiences I had been shown of the brotherhood, but about an intense grief I was feeling toward my wife. I had the feeling she had passed away and I was mourning her death.

I knew it was something that was either happening in the future or in a past life, but it felt as if it were very present. I realize now that these hallucinogens from the Psilocybin Mushrooms remove our ego, or perhaps create a space where there is no ego, allowing us to feel our raw emotions and access our deepest psychic ability.

I was overwhelmed with sadness. I don't remember how long I cried. I'll never forget the intensity of the grief and feeling I was seeing an event to come, or an event that had occurred. I know my wife and I have lived many lifetimes together. To this day I don't know which of them I may have been witnessing while experiencing that grief.

Energy has always been a large part of the brotherhood's process. On Saturday mornings, when we began the official part of our program, we always sat in a circle, having smudged ourselves with sage and lit a candle in the center of the circle.

During this time, each member knew he had the right to speak, (as we never had a leader) to pray or to say whatever was on his mind. This was/is an official calling in of the energies. Often times silence was the case. Requests, blessings, prayers and chanting often occurred.

Another practice during this circle is the practice of inhaling the breath together as a group. Sometimes three breaths, sometimes more, there isn't any set order to this process. We begin our Sunday morning in exactly the same way. We have come to see it as the official beginning of our work. After the circle is complete, we often share whatever experience we have had.

This lends a structure to what we do and it also establishes the energy in the space where we meet. Specifically, it is a form of asking for our guides, teachers and light beings to join us. Other members may interpret it differently; however, that is my experience.

The energy of our group has grown over the years and we believe it is advantageous to meet in the same place repeatedly for that reason. Jack Winner's wife, Jeannie Winner, has graciously allowed us the use of their home for a number of years now. Her willingness to leave for an entire weekend is and has been deeply appreciated. We usually take up a collection of money and Jack purchases flowers for Jeannie to show our appreciation. Jeannie is truly a special person.
I have also come to realize what a special person Jack Winner is. Jack is the epitome of a late bloomer. Jack never seems to age. Having known him for 20 years, the only outward appearance of him that seems to have changed is the color of his hair. On the inside, however, Jack has changed in huge ways. Jack always spoke so quickly I could barely understand him. When he gets excited, his rate of speech increases. Henry David Thoreau said, "Men lead lives of quiet desperation." I could always feel the seething sort of quiet desperation burning inside Jack Winner. There was always a dissatisfaction of what was taking place and a desire for something different. Jack looked for what wasn't there, instead of what was. He would constantly place attention on improving his own health, our health and our perspective.

Whereas, the spiritual side of things and the bigger picture always came to me easily, Jack seemed to struggle with it. Like a scientist, he was always looking for proof, always searching for the answer.

I know no one on this planet who is more committed to their success than Jack. When he determined that the Chiron Brotherhood didn't serve his needs, he had no regrets and wasted no time leaving our group.

Six years later, upon reconvening, his return to the Chiron Brotherhood astounded and surprised me. I can only attribute his re-entry into our group as a committed effort on his part to find the answer to whatever he sought.

Jack never failed to apprise the group of his newest discoveries on health, techniques to achieve it and knowledge. He is an innovator, one who takes different current modalities and jostles them together to create a new one.

Always a quick thinker, Jack delights in reporting his success stories as a chiropractor, which is his profession. Jack has also taught me that great change can occur in each of us. He has helped me see that we can heal the issues with our families, specifically, our fathers, and move on.

I admire Jack's tenacity, persistence and dedication to his own success. He continually does everything he can to improve his ability to help other people and himself. Although, I find Jack to be extremely perceptive, he, like Colin, believes he is not that energy-sensitive.

He is consistently working on this, and I've seen great changes take place in his ability to delineate energy. He could always do it in people, now he's doing it in rooms, spaces and buildings.

The most shocking memory I have about Jack is hearing a conversation where he purportedly told his wife, Jeannie that we had invited women to join the Chiron Brotherhood. As unthinkable as that possibility is, I could actually imagine Jack having made that statement to his wife.

Throughout the years, I believe their relationship has had some very fiery moments. Just as Jack's personality has its fiery sides, I imagine Jeannie may have hers as well.

Jack now hosts the Chiron Brotherhood weekend experiences. His generosity in opening their home and his wife's willingness to vacate for the weekend create the sanctuary where we meet. He has always welcomed us with open arms and has mentioned on numerous occasions the benefit and the energy of having the Chiron Brotherhood meet in his home. His hospitality and his flexibility are without bounds.

As have the rest of us, Jack has changed tremendously over the years. His intensity is now balanced with a certain level of contemplation. Jack is grounded, wise in the ways not only of the physical body, but open to new experiences. A family man, Jack has always supported his children and his wife. The change I see in Jack is that now he is also supporting himself. He is careful to assess his own needs and is not hesitant to make those needs known.

In the past, he, like Colin, would remain quiet until the pressure cooker had to blow. Now he is quicker to make a contribution to the conversation and to speak his piece. He has become more confident and stronger in his desire to make a contribution to our group. I believe that the desire was always there, though it was tempered with insecurity as to whether or not the contribution would be accepted.

102

Jack recently demonstrated his openness by asking me to clear the energy in his office, an old antebellum mansion on one of the main streets of Gainesville, Georgia. His curiosity piqued when I discovered several energies in the house that I felt needed to leave in order to raise the vibrational frequency of the building.

Jack was most curious about how this would be done and encouraged the process all the way. The Jack Winner I knew 20 years ago would never have offered himself that experience or me that privilege. I am grateful to have Jack in my life today.

I am reminded of an incident early on in the Brotherhood's evolution. Having terminated our weekend on a Sunday afternoon, a birthday party was to take place immediately afterward. I was in the basement where we often met in Farra's home on Lake Lanier, near Gainesville. Unbeknownst to me, a woman who was doing some catering had entered the house and was downstairs preparing food. I felt a kind of shock, almost as if an invasion had occurred. I practically ran upstairs. I told someone that a woman had entered the house and was assured that she had permission to do so.

Though it is not a reflection on the woman, I will never forget the sense of intrusion I felt as a result of her presence. This is a testimonial to the energy that is established whenever the Chiron Brotherhood meets. It is not an egotistical or prideful comment, nor is it meant to be. It is simply my experience that when we come together, a very powerful energy and chemistry is created. It is proof of the trust, reverence, and cooperation that exists in our group. Once again, it is appropriate to express gratitude to our members and to Spirit and the energy that is present during our activities.

The aspect of sexuality has played a huge part over the years in our involvement with the Chiron Brotherhood. I am not speaking of sexuality amongst our members. To my knowledge, that has never happened. As far as I know, everyone in the group is heterosexual. I am speaking of the discussion of sexual activity and its effect on those of us in the group.

There are men in the group for whom sexuality seems to be a driving force. These men we have labeled physical sexuals. The other contingent is labeled emotional sexuals. The difference is in the amount of libido that each individual experiences and demonstrates. For the physical sexuals in the group, of which I am one, sexuality is a large driving force. For the emotional sexuals, it appears that libido is not such an important aspect of life. It was Colin Tipping, now the successful author of the Radical Forgiveness series of books, who pointed this out to us.

The first thing that impressed me about Colin was his English accent. I never tired of listening to him speak.

Colin was a Realtor when I met him and not a very successful one. His struggles in life revolved around money. He wanted to be successful and he worked hard at it, however, it never seemed, in those early days, to bless him with its presence.

Colin had been a fully tenured professor in England. In great contrast to Farra, George and myself, Colin didn't seem to have much interest or drive in the area of sex.

His wife, JoAnn, was introduced to me at one of the Peace Gatherings at the home of Rick and Jeni Prigmore, founders of Universal Brotherhood Movement.

Colin, like myself, George Poirier and Dennis McCauley were ordained Ministers with UBM. Jack Winner and Farra Allen eventually obtained their ordination as well. I remember Colin asking me at one of those peace gatherings if I could help him with his migraine headaches. I went inside my own mind and asked if there were anything I could do. The answer was, "No" and I related that answer to Colin. He was clearly disappointed and later at one of our Chiron Brotherhood meetings, pointed out to me how angry he was about my answer.

Colin's education and his knowledge impressed me. He was an enigma to me, in that; I had met very few men who did not have great interest in sexuality. It was eye-opening to listen to a man talk, who was not that interested in sex. To me it was even stranger that he was married to a woman I considered to be attractive.

My observation of Colin was that even when heated arguments took place in our group, he would often sit quietly, with little to say, even though I could see the wheels turning behind his eyes. He knew a great deal more than he was letting on.

Colin could sit for very long periods of time, simply observing a conversation that was taking place amongst other men, without making a verbal contribution. I never believed for a moment that he didn't have something to say, but for some reason he was reluctant to speak. He was always calm, collected and proper. His clothing was always formal and clean, never a hair out of place, never a piece of clothing awry, always well groomed and always very courteous.

What was missing was happiness. I don't remember Colin smiling very much in the early days. The first time I saw Colin express anger in our group, I was shocked. He never appeared to me to be an angry individual. In retrospect, I can see that there was a lot brewing under the surface, quite like a pressure cooker.

In one of our meetings, he became very angry and very verbal. To my surprise, his mannerism, expression and delivery shocked the group. I no longer remember the subject that fueled his anger, but I could see that it had been brewing for a long time. Colin's greatest concern for many years seemed to be his lack of prosperity.

To this day, I believe him to be one of the men most changed by his participation in the Chiron Brotherhood. He went from a position of great scarcity to a position of tremendous success and prosperity.

He is also instrumental, from my perspective, in helping the group keep clear direction. He is a very task oriented individual and is incredibly consistent in his attention to detail. This has undoubtedly helped him throughout the years to manage and maintain the success that he has achieved.

One of Colin's greatest gifts is his ability to listen to a person's story quietly and then offer brilliant feedback. The logical expression of his thoughts and his ability to delineate alternatives for individuals have clearly helped him in his counseling and his writing.

Colin consistently expressed his lack of sensitivity when it came to energy and energy work. His impression of himself, I should imagine, was as a very left brained logical individual. I found it difficult to believe that a man as clear as Colin did not have the sensitivity I felt he had.

Colin consistently reminded us to accept whatever was taking place in our lives, regardless of how annoying the challenge. I remember an allegory I once heard, where people were described as differing kinds of horses. There were race horses, thoroughbreds, draft horses, quarter horses, miniature horses, and a few others I can't remember. Colin always struck me as a workhorse, moving steadily along the row, plowing the future for possibilities and opportunities. His determination and persistence always impressed me. To this day, I believe him to be one of the most prolific men I've ever met.

I was jealous of Colin's success until I began to accept myself, in a more complete way. Secretly, perhaps, I am still jealous.

Colin has also found a level of comfort in that prosperity. He is definitely a happier man. I admire Colin's ability to get the job done with determination and persistence.

His self-discipline is amazing. Colin is always looking for ways to improve his work. Even when it seems as if it couldn't get any better, he's looking for changes to make. He has taught me the concept of sticking to the task until it is completed. I have also learned from Colin to limit the number of tasks I take on, thereby not over committing myself. More importantly, I have learned from Colin to believe in myself and move forward.

Regardless of our interest or lack thereof, sex is frequently a topic in our gathering conversations. I imagine that if there were no physical sexuals in the group, the topic would seldom be discussed.

For over 20 years, I have been faithful to my wife, Sandra, this being my second marriage and her third. Whereas, I had been promiscuous in my first marriage, experiencing four extra – marital sexual encounters, I have come to realize how important loyalty to a partner is.

I have altered my behavior in this relationship, having learned how painful the guilt of promiscuity can be, not only for my partner, but for me. Although I am faithful to my wife, as referred to earlier in my reflections, I have lived vicariously through the descriptions of other members' experiences. I have often found those experiences exciting to listen to, and have definitely experienced jealousy around them, given my ability to fantasize.

Not only has our group discussed the differing libidos between partners, we have also discussed the change in the libido that happens over the years, for both men and women. As we age, our libidos shift, based on a number of factors.

Being a physical sexual my libido has not decreased. I don't know if that is the case with most men who are physicals. I only know that, for me, the desire is not only there, but seems to be as strong as ever.

This creates a great challenge, both in my work and my life. A large percentage of my clientele are female. I must admit that I have often had to suppress my feelings for clients, acquaintances and other women. One learns to rise above such feelings in order to practice monogamy, loyalty and what I deem to be appropriate behavior for myself.

Over the years, it has become easier and my relationship with my wife is more important than any acting out I may have done previously. Therefore, respectful, appropriate behavior becomes the only acceptable behavior for me. Undoubtedly, it is the safety I feel in the men's groups I am involved in, which allows me to discuss the issue. There is little risk in any unfortunate outcome, when experiencing that safety and being able to vent those feelings through conversation, with those whom I feel no danger.

Over the years, my own wife, Sandie, has often vacated our home in order for the Brotherhood or another of my men's groups to meet, without feminine presence. Sandie has been extremely supportive of my men's group work. I can tell that having a safe place to express and to receive feedback has taken a lot of pressure off of her.

Were I not involved in men's work, she would probably receive the brunt of my emotions; good, bad or ugly. It has been a Godsend over the years to receive the support of my brothers in these groups, and to feel as though I am not judged, based on who I am, what I do, or what I say.

As men and women, we have a choice to create a safe place, a group of people, and a support group, whatever you wish to call it, where we can express ourselves and expect nothing less. It is invaluable to my sanity to know that I can depend on my Chiron Brothers and the men in my local men's group whenever I need safe space. I would say to those who judge my comments to be sexist, that they are not. I would encourage every woman to find a similar support group, or create it, if necessary, in order to experience the same level of acceptance.

I am reminded of my grandfathers, both on my father's side, and mother's side. From my perspective, these men, whom I loved dearly, did not express their emotions easily, if ever. I know they both loved me, yet they showed that love in a way that was stoic, to say the least. As the years rolled on, my own father became more emotionally expressive, but in the early days his ability to express was extremely limited.

We have the opportunity to teach our sons, our grandsons, our daughters and our granddaughters that emotional expression is safe. We can teach them that it is safe to love one another, to create groups where that love can be freely expressed, and therefore, to live our lives meaningfully, with a high level of sanity, the freedom to express, and a sense of trust around it. In my opinion, we should expect nothing less, and we have a responsibility to ourselves and those around us to do so.

My Reflections on Being Part of the Chiron Brotherhood

by Farra Allen

I am really excited to recount my life-altering experience with my Chiron Brothers. Let me first start with the background.

As to the outer background, initially our setting was on a 25 acre wooded lakefront lot complete with trails throughout. Situated at the very end of the lake it was private, beautiful, and tranquil. I had rented a nice large, expensive house there. This was what I felt I needed as I was coming off the roughest time of my life. I had just undergone a divorce with the woman who I thought was my Soul Mate and had lost my *baby*, so to speak - the Atlanta School of Massage.

This school was my creation, my life's work and it was extraordinary. It was widely considered to be one of the best massage schools in the country, and at the time it certainly was.

Needless to say when wanting to work out a *win-win* agreement, I was crushed when my wife and partner at the time said, "Buy, sell or I'll bankrupt your f_ _ _ing ass and believe me, I know how."

113

There were times when I felt like ending it all and many times I'd lay in bed curled up with my little West Highland Terrier, Baby Girl. Thank God for her.

I had been the personality, visionary, and spiritual leader creating a New Age, mind/body community around my school and all of a sudden I was alone. Scared and wondering how I was going to make a living, I was living in survival mode.

My ex-wife was now owner of the school and since she had been the business brain behind the enterprise all along, I had to sell and get committed to finding out what it takes to have a life of fulfillment. This brought up tremendous angst and consternation in me.

I recount this to show that this was my inner landscape when we first gathered together in 1994, the same year I got divorced and lost my most precious baby - my school.

My new friend, George Poirier, had been sharing with me his vision of a men's group and all of a sudden one day they all arrived at my place and that was the start. As I recall, there were about 10 of us originally and early on a few came and went.

We then settled into our core group. George and our friend Dennis had initially invited most of the men and some came together quite spontaneously.

One day George and I were out on my boat and we ran into an acquaintance of mine rowing in the lake. She said, "I want you two to meet someone." We followed her to a nearby dock. When we met Jack Winner, who was to become a key player in our journey, we immediately felt a connection and he was invited.

So, we all met in my home and right away we engaged in confrontation and power struggles. Almost as if we had been an *argument waiting to happen*. I know I was insecure and out to look good and prove myself early on. I was also used to and comfortable with confronting and arguing. After all, I had completed law school and now had my opportunity to put my skills to the test. I was up against a formidable opponent in George Poirier, who was one of the most intelligent and well-read persons I have ever met.

We bantered over the leadership of the group. Initially, the battle seemed to revolve around his desire to bring new people into the group. While I had someone in mind too, my intuition and better sense told me this would not work. We had already bonded and we were naturally aligned with the vision of being vulnerable and honest with each other.

It seemed then, and still does now that this was the group that was to be together and was a fit. And, sure enough, this is how it turned out. For some unknown reason, we were the ones who were meant to be together, and try as we may to integrate new ones into the group, it never worked out - mostly because we were *the real deal*. This is to say we were committed to coming every weekend. (George and I never missed one over the 20-year span.) Initially, we would gather from Friday late afternoon until Sunday noontime every 6-8 weeks like clockwork.

We had many highlights, one of them being our sweat lodge experience. Someone came up with a Lakota Pipe Carrier, who led us in a real deal sweat. It was really intense and some brothers had trouble with it. We cut the trees down and built the lodge in the morning over my birthday weekend early on in our time together. This was really special. The experience of collectively sharing in a non-verbal manner was very bonding for us, both individually and as a group.

Every event was special in its own way and we never knew what would happen as we never had an agenda. We just got together and hung out. We then opened the focused part of the day Saturday morning, with an opening ritual which brought us into the oneness of our collective energy. Through this ritual, we raised the consciousness of the group with each of us becoming more than our individual egos. We became intuitive channels for what needed to be said in the moment. This was, to me, a rare and special ritual. The feeling of connectedness would remain with us throughout the weekend.

After the ritual was over, we began the work. We would take turns checking in and then, with no set agenda, begin the processing

The processing was challenging for me and possibly others, too as most of us were used to having a plan. Going into something not knowing was unnerving at times. In addition, we had to have consensus on all group decisions and this led to long and laborious heated arguments since I and some others, no doubt, had an investment in doing it *my way.*

I had a good history of relating to men. However, it tended to revolve around athletics since I was always playing sports. Later on I tended towards relating to women as they seemed less intimidating and more nurturing, which I felt I needed at the time.

So, being able to hang out with these men, powerful and successful healers themselves, was challenging and ultimately healing for me. I began to experience that I had something to offer these men as I shared with them quite a bit when processing and I felt like I held my own. This tended to give me more confidence and self-esteem as these were no slouchers.

As a result, my relationships with the individuals grew and expanded. We came to appreciate each other for the unique special gifts we all are. Comparison and competition, while initially prevalent, subsided and eventually dissipated.

Now what is left is respect and love for each other. After all, we are the ones who have hung in through thick and thin and, believe me, there were those times. Overall, it has been a truly remarkable life altering journey.

Just the fact of a men only meeting like this was great for all of us. I feel it is valuable for each gender to do. My partner, Marion, quite often leaves me and goes off with her girlfriends with my blessings. There is something quite healing and nurturing about being with only those of your own sexual gender. It benefits both partners.

As to our unique group, we were serious in our intentions to grow. Personally, I knew this was what I needed which was to own my own power and feel like I could launch my own business by myself and make a living. My life depended on this so I tended to have a little passion about making sure others were as committed, not only in showing up, but also in busting their ass while there.

The work we did was not for the faint-at-heart by any means. We thrust elbows into each other. I even drew blood on one occasion as I went through a rage session. This particular session was a highlight for me as I had suppressed tremendous rage surrounding my relationship with my father who was a rageaholic.

Finally, I had an opportunity to express this emotion and when I did, it was a release I will never forget, and hugely healing. In fact, this was the course of the day, as we did tremendous healing with each other. If one guy didn't confront you, another would and there was no hiding. I felt trepidation and tension. However, I knew I needed to be there AND not back down on anything and this is the way we went about it. Of course, George was all about this and he had clearly established himself as our leader by this time.

So we would take turns sharing and then we would tag team process each other leaving ***nothing*** left over. One of us would see something and confront the person speaking while the others would actively listen for whatever else needed to be said. Again, hiding out was not an option.

Some could not handle the heat and we dwindled down to the five of us that still remain *the true core*. We had created a safe container for us to be able to go through whatever we each needed to go through and, believe me, we all did it.

As we continued to share deeply, openly, intimately, vulnerably and honestly, we faced any and all that we needed to face. This continued to be what we always did until we finally reached a point wherein we began to feel complete. Then we tended to switch over to only addressing what popped up when taking turns checking in.

All of us were, and are, highly intuitive, intelligent, mindful, present, insightful, and supportive of each other. Although, this was not always the case. As a result, each and every weekend we met has produced outstanding results for each of us.

We also spent and spend time just hanging out and talking about whatever subject comes up in the conversation. Around meals and after our daylong meeting, this is what we do and it bonds and nourishes us. I tend to appreciate some of this time more than others depending upon the nature of the conversation we engage in. Many times it has to do with sexual subjects on which each of us has our own take.

Certainly, sexual addiction had been an issue of mine as I had an Oedipal Complex with my mother. My dad was not all that happy about that, so she pulled away from our relationship. For me, the only thing that seemed to fill the void left was getting laid.

This has changed dramatically and the group has been a huge part of my healing as I now have a great fulfilling relationship of 14+ years together. For that, I say thanks to our Chiron Brotherhood.

Before that, I acted out and in fact one time when we were meeting together one real hot number showed up at my home. I took a break and ducked into my bedroom searching for my next fix. I didn't get it. However, it did cause disruption and anger in the group as you might imagine.

I admittedly was deeply damaged, both from childhood and from the fresh loss of my school. My progress seemed too slow for Jack, who felt he had it more together than me and was tired of the same old story. As a result, one day Jack announced he was leaving the group. This was in December, 1996.

I went ballistic and started throwing water bottles all over my house where we held the meeting in Virginia Highlands in Atlanta. Jack had been such a close ally and had really been there for me, so I felt betrayal and bewilderment. This caused a break in our meetings and there was a period of time before we reconvened in August of 2000.

However, George and I never lost the vision. I think Greg held it, too, and certainly Colin did as the Brotherhood had dramatically altered his life. I know by this time Colin just appreciated getting together as we had bonded and it was healing just to hang out together. We had shared something extremely profound.

Colin and I had finally owned our power amongst strong, powerful men without needing to prove or dominate or control. This, my friends, was life-altering. The relationships we had formed will always be there.

Seven years later Jack came back to us and, in fact, offered up his wonderful home for us to meet on Lake Lanier, which was close to our original home. In the meantime, he had built a glassed in high ceiling room overlooking the lake. It was perfect for our Spiritual opening time together as we meditated, chanted, channeled, held hands and connected on all levels. This was spiritually uplifting for me. Greg, especially, carried the energy for us in this aspect of our getting together and invariably bringing in other energies. I always really look forward to this as it seems a necessary part of who we are and who we will be.

Most recently, Jack engaged fully and worked through some deep emotional issues himself, saying that he was judgmental about me having such issues. This is what many people do, men and women alike. When the wound is deep, we tend to hide. As George always says, "Never underestimate the power of denial."

Well, Jack finally let it rip and we are all back together now; the *real deal core five*.

Of those who have come and gone, two are deceased, some were asked to leave, others took it upon themselves to exit. We now get together twice a year normally and still gain great benefit in doing so. Colin went from bankruptcy to driving a

121

Jaguar in addition to traveling the world doing his work and producing a huge following. He is our poster child. However, the impact has been enormous for all of us.

Greg is a world renowned trans channel who continually travels to Europe to conduct his work. George is our Spiritual Monk and astrological wiz along with being the glue that holds us all together and keeps on being our midwife, so to speak, birthing and rebirthing us.

Jack has a big beautiful mansion for a Wellness Center in downtown Gainesville with a great business and a great relationship with his wife, just as we all do now.

And me, well, I finally got my shit together and in 2006 started my next school, LifeWorks School of Coaching where I train and certify life coaches. In addition, I have a strong coaching practice specializing in working with young men. I call them fledgling adults.

Clearly, this tight-knit group has been life altering if not life-saving for me. I love who I am now and I experience my wholeness and self-acceptance; a gift for which I am forever grateful.
In conclusion, and for the benefit of those of you reading this book, this is what our Chiron Brotherhood has taught me:

> • Be vulnerable, become aware, allow yourself to acknowledge your shadow.
> • Find your spiritual connection, practice and trust in Spirit.

• Express your emotions fully and don't hold back. The release is deeply healing.
• Create a safe environment to air out your dirty laundry
• Be radically honest in your interactions with others in a loving and compassionate way.
• It is possible to have and create deep meaningful connections with those of the opposite sex without having sex.
• And lastly, persevere. We all had bumps along the road. However, we were the ones who stayed the course; we were committed and thus, we got the ransom. Go for it, you can do it too in your own unique, beautiful way.

My Perceptions of My Chiron Brothers:

Greg:
I liked Greg the first time I met him. He carried himself with grace and dignity, clearly implying to me that he was confident and successful. I was impressed and interested to get to know him. Greg spoke very well as he shared in the group, choosing his words carefully and always portraying a strong presence.

At the same time, I had a difficult time experiencing a strong connection with Greg. At one point, I traveled up to Boone, N.C., where he lived and hoped to connect, but did not. As I think more about it, Greg reminds me of my Dad in a way, as he too seemed to have a strong sense and confidence in himself while remaining somewhat aloof.

I have always admired and appreciated how Greg carried himself. He is a strong leader with excellent leadership skills as well as an effective, successful businessman. Focused, hard-working, caring deeply about other people, a great healer, skilled in many facets of his work, he is a force to be reckoned with. Greg has helped many a soul on the path through his devotion and commitment to people.

Living quite a distance from the rest of us, Greg had the farthest to drive and, out of his strong commitment to our group, almost always made the trip down. He really saw the value of us getting together and you could count on Greg being fully present once he made it down to us. More than anyone, I saw him as our spiritual leader. He would bring in our Spirit Guides which always enhanced the quality of our interactions. I always wanted him around for that, along with the fact that he always came with a smile and a positive attitude. I love the guy.

What I found most enigmatic about Greg is while he was usually fully present in our meetings, he would literally fall asleep when I was sharing. I did not exactly see that as a positive characteristic for such a powerful healer. I think he became weary of me continuing to deal with my father issues and lost patience with me. I also found it strange that while he would appear to connect with me deeply upon arriving at the meetings, he would also become aloof as mentioned above.

Like all of us, Greg has changed a lot. I now feel his connection with me and his love coming to me which is awesome. He is now finding time for himself, swimming a lot, using his hot tub, riding his motorcycle, and many other enjoyable activities that leave him a lot more balanced. Furthermore, he is more committed to the group than ever before as there were some times that he missed. We can all feel the presence that he brings which is even more evident than ever before. He, like all of us, is more at peace within himself and it shows.

I have learned to be more focused on business from Greg, and to balance myself. I am more hard working than before, more grounded, stronger spiritually, and I can say that from being around Greg he has been a positive influence for me in all of these most important areas.

I have learned the value of being a stabilizing force for other people through Greg and I have learned that, while one may appear to be a certain way, I don't have to take that personal and feel bad about me. For all of this, I am a better man for having met and had Gregg in my life for the past twenty years.

George:

My *Bro*. I first met George at Joyce and Dennis's home in the mountains and we had an immediate connection. (Both of them were graduates of my massage school.)

My first impressions: George was a strong presence, he owned his power fully. I always looked up to George somewhat and have been impressed by him. Early on, even though we had formed a quick and fast friendship, we had some control dramas in our group. Both being natural leaders, George and I bumped heads on who was going to set the direction of the group. Nevertheless, even though we might have yelled at each other, it was all in good spirit. I always have respected George and think highly of him.

I admire George in many ways. I especially have appreciated how George has kept his own confidence and self-esteem high in the absence of years of low-income productivity. He remains the same guy and all of us know that we can count on him to be fully there for us.

George clearly has owned the leadership of our group and continues to do so. He has always been the most committed and the most involved, in all ways. While he has had his own bouts with addictions and other various issues, he has always been available to every person in the group, including me. George and I remain the only ones never to have missed one single meeting in all our time together.

Feeling how solid he is in that way has always been a good feeling for me. It enhances my safety level and it has gone a long way in keeping this group together for 20 years. You cannot slip something by him as he is like a hawk; he watches and listens intently and deeply. If I was encountering any difficulty or avoiding anything, he would confront and challenge me, sometimes strongly. He, more than anyone, was always committed to getting past wherever I was stuck and he stopped at nothing in his endeavor to push me there.

That is the epitome of commitment to another human being. George became my roommate for a period of time as well. He was always there for me as an emotional support, which of all his qualities, I would say, is his best quality. He is there like a rock for me and I always know and feel it.

Again, this brings safety and a soft spot in my heart for my brother (he feels like the brother I never had). I am indebted to George for starting the men's group and keeping it together; clearly the glue. He has been and continues to be a much appreciated support to my continued personal growth as well as a teacher who has greatly influenced my personal life and my work.

As you can see I appreciate George for a lot. I can also say that out of who he has been, I have learned to *be* a whole lot of that, too. I have brought much of this into my coaching and my training of others. The body/mind approaches that George demonstrated have influenced my work greatly as well as all that I have mentioned. In looking back all these years and reflecting upon all that has occurred I am struck by how much I have been influenced merely by who these individuals are and who they will be.

That said, all of us have enigmatic qualities. Regarding George, I found it interesting that while he seemed to be so positive and charismatic and a visionary, he would at times be the *naysayer* with me. For instance, when I told him I was starting a coaching school he flat out said, "No way that's going to fly, Bro."

While it was a formidable task, I have made it fly and clearly he was overly pessimistic. In a similar way when I met Marion and told him I was sold on her, he not only objected and said, "No way will that work," he even brought in the other brothers to have a kind of intervention with me to convince me otherwise. Marion and I are together 14+ years and getting better by the day.

As to changes for George, once I introduced the concept of radical honesty to the group, George tucked that ball into his belly and ran with it. The personal changes he has made have been enormous, going through a 12-step program, and now having a relationship where he is, for the first time, monogamous is a huge shift. Moving away from his calling as a *real deal healer* that he is and being satisfied living the life of a monk in some ways with two strong women is an enormous change for him. He, nevertheless, wears it well.

Colin:

Early on, I gravitated towards Colin quite a bit as I felt his trepidation and I too was intimidated somewhat by such strong men. Given the domination I felt from my dad, I shrank backwards and always felt a kinship with Colin. At that time, I felt most like Colin in the sense that we each felt a certain lack of confidence and true personal power. At the time, Colin was struggling financially and even filed bankruptcy.

As he began to own his power and assert himself, his life seemed to take off like a bat out of Hell. Clearly he is our poster child and once he owned his power in our group along with the private work George did with him, he took off.

Professionally, Colin stayed very focused, always a hard worker. Once he believed in himself, his business exploded. He is a great writer, a *real deal healer*, and has made a huge impact on a great number of people especially with his work on forgiveness of others and self-forgiveness. In this area, he is a maverick and we all look up to him. He is always a nice guy and easy for me to be with although our connection has been primarily limited to our group. Watching Colin get his professional life together was great. We all felt part of his success.

As to what I found most enigmatic about Colin: I always questioned whether he was totally honest about being happy with his personal life. He didn't appear to me to have what I thought a man would want and, in fact, need in his committed relationship. I don't know how much that had to do with what would make me happy and the disparity there as to what may be just fine with him. At any rate, he seems fine now with what he has.

Changes abound for Colin, many of which I have already alluded to. One of the weekends when we were up in Boone at Greg's home, it appeared to me that he was a natural teacher and I confronted him about it. In fact, we all kept on him about it, so he did a presentation on Radical Forgiveness to the group and showed up in a big way. I saw the spark in his eyes and face as he demonstrated on a whiteboard.

He has become the epitome of professional change and personal transformation greatly assisted by his Chiron Brothers, especially George, who took a personal interest in Colin and did some coaching with him outside the group. Needless to say, we are proud of our brother Colin.

I have learned much from Colin, especially business focus, the value of hard work, writing skills and hunkering down to business. Also, he has been a teacher through observing his empathy for others, his commitment to forgiveness (which I teach in my school and with my clients), his integrity, his love for people, etc. I am blessed by being around such people. I learn and grow as I become more of who they are and then demonstrate in my own life the positive qualities and attributes they possess.

Jack:

Once again, I always loved this guy, too. Soon after moving up to Gainesville, I met Jack and he immediately treated me like family. This was really important to me as I was displaced quite a bit after selling the Atlanta School of Massage, and leaving and missing all my friends and the community I had forged. He and his wife would even invite my son and I to come to their home for holidays. We spent social time together outside of the group.

I admired Jack for many other things as well. Dr. Jack Winner was another strong healer and powerful man, a successful businessman who was focused and grounded, probably more than anyone in the group. He is warm, loving, fun and joking, generous, bright, skillful, well rounded, has a great relationship (now), strong in many, many ways, has a holistic healing center in the heart of Gainesville, is active in his community, in his family etc. etc. As you can see, we have some great men here.

What I found most enigmatic about him was when I traded sessions with Jack; me doing coaching on him and he doing chiropractic on me. As to his work, I have always felt that, though it worked initially, it seemed temporary and he did not go to the source like the rest of us did. He seemed to like

130

coming to the group quite a bit but, at the time, he did not fully engage in the deep healing processes the rest of us were doing.

After two years of hearing the same story from me, as I was stuck in my stuff at the time, Jack announced he was leaving the group. I went ballistic and started throwing water bottles and screaming at him. I could not imagine Jack leaving as he had been a real integral part of the group and an important person in my life. Furthermore, he had violated my high value of commitment, one in which he claimed to have himself. While appearing to be the real deal like the rest of us, Jack had been evasive and avoided confronting what he most needed to do for himself.

That said, there were many changes. After a number of years, not only did Jack come back to the group, he offered up his home for us to meet. This has been the perfect setting for us right on Lake Lanier and Jack has finally done the level of deep healing work that, as a healer, he needed to do. Furthermore, his work now is long-lasting and impacts the emotional body more perhaps than it has before.

Timing is everything and forgiveness is key here too as we are all back to where we were originally with him. Jack had been evasive at times and avoided confronting himself fully, but no longer. This has increased my respect and appreciation of him. We are all deeply indebted to him and his wife Jeannie, for hosting us as well. All is well that ends well and this story has a good ending.

What I have learned from Jack: Once again all of what I mention as to my appreciations of Jack. Let's face it, there is no accident that he lives on a magnificent piece of property smack on the best part of the lake and that he is strong financially. The focus on business and success and groundedness has rubbed off on me and I am forever grateful for having had the opportunity to be influenced for 20 years by him and all the other men.

This has been our core. In summary, one could not get by with hiding one iota since, if one person did not catch it, another would, and we always confronted. This was instrumental in my development as I give each of them credit for empowering me, healing me and enabling me to literally transform many lives as a result of the support I always received from these four powerful men.

It was not always what I wanted and yet always what I needed and without a doubt they each in their own individual way have assisted me to experience my own wholeness, my authentic self and lead many others to this same important destination.

This group has evolved and altered many lives in the past two decades through our gatherings, first intense and confrontative, always supportive and giving each of us what we needed most which we have now passed forward to many others. Hopefully to you, the reader, as well. So be it.

My Reflections on Being Part of the Chiron Brotherhood

by Jack Winner

I remember when the group first got together, the battles were more verbal with George, Farra and maybe Greg and Dennis. Some of us; Colin, Jack and Gerry were trying to sort out what this experience was all about and what it meant to each of us. Thank goodness there was a consensus because we quieter ones were probably not going to take control of the direction. Personally I was just sitting in the experience and watching to see if I could align with the groups direction.

The first major point of contention with us was about staying for the weekend. This was major for me. I felt committed and accountable for myself and the group. Though I didn't understand where this whole group was going, I knew trusting one another was monumental. To me leaving the group short of our three days together breached the trust. George and Farra probably spearheaded that issue, but I felt others of us, as a whole, supported that mindset.

These confrontations were continuous over our years together. I also believe they were the glue that held us together. This statement is almost a dichotomy, as the more we pushed on each other, the more we created a bond. The more powerful each of us was, it added a stronger energy to the group. It was not my intention, nor was it anyone's in the group, to embarrass or disrespect, judge or criticize any other man. Yet, that had been how most of us had been raised. Society has been using that for generations to establish positions of force and power. Now, through some kind of intervention, we had men maintain their power and use it to empower others. These confrontations were necessary for each of us to understand and reestablish our own power and add it to the group. Over time, this synergism expanded our group in ways we could not understand or imagine in the beginning.

As time progressed, we talked about bringing other men into our group; I felt conflicted. I liked and trusted our established group members and felt secure. I still had a lot of fears and esteem issues I wasn't ready or yet able to bring to our group, let alone bring some new guys in who might not be so kind. Also, I felt we had a powerful group and felt protective of our success and wasn't sure I wanted to give it away to someone else. To heck with them. We worked hard to get here. It would be hard to bring them up to the level we have struggled to get to.

The other side of the coin is if this is how it can work for us could it work for the rest of society? Could we all hold to the core elements of trust, respect, caring and loving attitude, and still work together and make *this world* a better place. A heaven here on earth? Wild thought, but I was willing to give it a chance and find out.

So new members, why not? I just swallowed hard and looked for the possibilities.

Another major issue that needed attention was the idea that there was not to be anyone else in the house while we were processing, and this was monumental. Trusting these men and feeling safe in our environment was a must. I know this issue with me goes back lifetimes for me. I had to know that my back was covered. In this group of like-minded and accountable men, it was.

In the Spring of 1996, I did not attend a group breathwork process that was held outside our intimate group, nor did I attend any other sessions outside of our group. In retrospect, I think I was fearful of engaging with others I did not know and trust in an environment I wasn't comfortable. I still had a lot of self-esteem issues and wasn't ready to deal with them yet and certainly didn't want to share them with people I didn't feel comfortable with or trust.

One of the topics of conversation in our group was sex. I enjoyed hearing about George and Farra's sexual encounters. It was fun, entertaining conversation. However, sex was not an issue with me or a few others of us in the group. What was good about this issue is that we did talk about it and it helped me desensitize it. As we worked with this issue over time, I came to appreciate sex and sexuality and enjoy it as the basic human need that it is.

Then there was the book on Radical Honesty. The book and topic ignited some core issues in all of us. Though sex was one of those issues, being totally honest was another. I remember Mike would not deal with some of his issues. He kept dodging and weaving around his issues. As he did this and each member kept trying to bring Mike to get real, Colin began brewing. The more Mike dodged and weaved, the more Colin became incensed. That was the first time I saw Colin's face get red and his demeanor dramatically changed. Finally, when Colin could take no more, he blew up at Mike. This incident was so climatic because it was the exact reason we all came together. To awaken the 'Giants' within. Colin finally had enough and Mike did his part by being the catalyst. It worked perfectly. After that day, Colin was never the same again. He was a notable force in the group and beyond in his personal and professional life as well. This to me was one of the true meanings of the group.

The book, *Radical Honesty,* proposed that we all do an inventory of our dark secrets and withholds to our spouses. I disagreed with the idea of revealing all of our sexual partners and thought that most of the group disagreed with George's desire to put this into action. In retrospect, it was the catalyst he needed to look at his issues. Again without this group I don't know how long it would have taken George to look at this issue. He did and with some prodding from Phil Hall, George faced his issues and has assumed even more of his personal power.

There was another issue that came about due to our group interaction, Neuro Linguistic Programing or NLP. I decided to take a course in NLP and informed some of the members of its benefits. However, as has been my pattern, I did not fully engage with those who decided to take the course, i.e. George, Farra and Phil, as to my intentions nor ask for or give them my full support. In retrospect, this had always been my pattern. Outside this group, I have never counted on anyone. I didn't care if George or Farra or Phil got involved in NLP. It was what I wanted to do. That is what I have done all my life. Though I have had lots of self-esteem issues, I am beginning to realize they were there because I wanted someone else to validate me. My dad, my brother and some religious group and later people who I wanted to be in a relationship with. I couldn't relate well so I gave my power away to be accepted. As I gained my self-esteem, life worked out for me as I looked less for recognition and more for inner peace and joy. This is not to say I do not want to be social and like to have fun, but if it doesn't happen, it is not life altering for me.

It was mentioned that this incident and the withdrawing from NLP was the beginning of my withdrawal from the men's group. As I reflect back, my reason was more about what I was learning and I felt what I was doing in NLP was wasting my time. You can call that egotistical or judgmental, but it wasn't to me. Somewhere early in my life I heard that different drum beat. I didn't ask for validation or support then. I still didn't at that time.

By December, 1996 I was sensing that we were not moving forward. We were going over the same issues without resolution. My deciding to leave this group was no small matter. The weekend that this happened was not planned out by me, other than I had to leave. I felt what had brought me to the group had gone as far as it could. If I didn't move on I was being dishonest to these men and more so to myself. I couldn't be okay with myself not dealing with my issues and it was hard to watch them continuing to struggle with theirs. I felt I had more to offer and wanted to contribute helping them move on, but the timing wasn't right. So I needed to move on.

The difficult part about that weekend was it was important to me that they understood how I felt. These guys were not part of a casual relationship for me and, though I did not interact socially with them, they were about the core of who I was. They were the closest I had ever gotten to be aligned with a group of powerful men. I hoped this experience would change my life and help me realize my real power.

That Saturday was a challenging day. I knew Farra was angry and George disappointed. We had done a lot together and been through a lot together. In the back of my mind was a glimmer of hope that something might be said or done to let me see something that I needed to look at. In retrospect, the timing wasn't right.

So during that last meeting I wanted to respect my brothers and let them complete what we needed to complete together. We always were there for each other and in my last meeting together I wanted to go out that way. When I left on Sunday afternoon, I felt empty. It was an unusual and foreign feeling. The emptiness was not in my head, it was all over my body. I didn't know if it was good or bad, a relief and a loss at the same time. I knew something significant in my life had just happened, but I didn't know what it meant or what was going to happen from there. As I had learned from the past, I just was going to trust the process.

As an afterthought, several members of this group mentioned **a strong** Karmic connection of our original group. From the beginning of our group, I was very naive. I did not know about Karma or past lives or channels or the angels or the Masters. But what I did know is that somehow or somewhere

I had been with this group of men at some time in the past. It wasn't the words that they said, it was how they resonated. It was who they were, spiritually. There was substance about this experience.

Over the next 10 years, I continued to work on my stuff. I was thinking about the group, but I made my choice. I had begun two different groups in my community. However, there was no glue to hold us together. I felt those groups wanted a leader and most of the people wanted to follow. I didn't want to lead and I didn't want to follow. I wanted each of us to be accountable to ourselves and accountable to the whole. I wanted the power of the synergy of a dynamic group. Those groups quietly disbanded.

In 2007 one of the Chiron Brothers, Phil Hall, stopped by to see me in April, a week before his death. We talked about George and Farra and what happened with the group. Again, here was Phil being a catalyst in reigniting old flames. Since Phil was a member of the Unity Church in Gainesville, GA I went to the memorial service.

When I spoke about him, it brought back the memories of what we all did together. And though this group of people at the church heard me, they really couldn't understand the shifts that had occurred in my life from Phil and these Chiron Brothers. Not too long afterward, George called me and we talked about getting back together. It wasn't a long discussion and didn't take a lot of thought. The conversation resembled talking with an old friend and a kindred spirit. He mentioned that the core group would like to get together again and how did I feel about that? I was interested in seeing everyone again.

Even more interested in being in that energy again. I did have one reservation in the back of my mind. If we didn't deal with our stuff and take accountability for our actions, I probability was not in it for the long haul.

At that first meeting, the atmosphere was different. The whole group had shifted. We no longer shoved fists through someones navel, rather we talked about issues and how we might solve them with a win-win perspective. Always using our group synergy to unravel core issues we began to identify core beliefs and thoughts. This was a gentler approach and much more spiritual and, I think, much more powerful. Each weekend still began with us spiritually and intentionality aligning with each other and our guides and teachers. However, this time I think we were all not as forceful in our delivery system, but more powerful individually and as a group. The consciousness of the group had expanded. I liked these guys and this new direction.

One weekend we decided to take the psychedelic mushrooms. This was new for Colin and me. We always wondered what it was like to be out of control, yet we knew we would be safe with George and Farra watching over us. It was a very happy releasing experience. I laughed a lot and felt free. I was very thankful for George and Farra setting and maintaining a controlled and safe environment for us. Though I don't need to do it again, I am happy to have felt that feeling. I can understand, more now, why someone might want to take drugs, especially if they are in pain, either emotional or physical.

One weekend there were just the three of us. Colin was in England. Greg had a motorcycle mishap on the way to our meeting. But, it turned out to be another great weekend. George had a chance to really talk about his astrology and I got a real sense of the power of astrology and George. I could see Farra was shifting more into his life coaching and things were beginning to come together for him as well. He seemed to me to be picking up more confidence in himself.

During that weekend I, however, had two major clarifications. George had a chance to experience what I wanted to convey to him ten years earlier; to take him back to a loss of his brother when he was very young. He had been carrying that hurt and loss for a long time. It had been affecting his life in ways he wasn't fully aware of until then. He retraced that earlier life experience, released it, cleared it and had closure.

I, on the other hand, had Farra and George help me go back to a time when my dad served in World War II Germany. Through his eyes, I experienced what an eighteen-year-old kid saw in the Auschwitz Concentration Camp in 1945. As my brothers held points and delved into painful areas of my body, I began to experience what my dad saw and smelled and felt as he walked into that camp. To say I cried is an understatement. Every cell in my body vibrated with disbelief, anger, pain, disgust, bereavement, horror . . . you name it. It came wave after wave. At each wave, I cried harder and deeper. I could see into the faces of lifeless people and piles of others who had no life any longer and the smell was horrendous. My crying just intensified to where I didn't know where it would end. Every cell of my body vibrated with every thought and feeling until finally I couldn't cry anymore. I just let go. In my mindset, I just let it go to God . . . and trusted he knew what he was doing then and now.

141

From that day on probably more doors opened then I could have realized. I understood my dad. An eighteen-year-old young man doesn't need to see or be a part of that experience. But if he did, I don't know how you could come back home and raise a family and be emotionally sound. Some ways he did, but not without some repercussions. My dad and I were not real close, but now I could see more clearly why. I also realized that while there are some very bad things happening in this world, I needed to trust in God and my fellow man that there is a bigger plan. My job was to stay accountable to myself and others, as well as trust the right and proper things will eventually prevail. This is now my life's pattern. My Chiron Brothers are continuing to hold that space.

My Perception of My Brothers

Dennis

A necessary piece for me in this group came through Dennis, one of our group members. In him, I saw my own of men, especially those in power. Most weekends together I could feel my insides shaking almost continually. I talked fast and mumbled my words. I couldn't even express myself well because my fear kept me from thinking full thoughts. And when everyone talked about a subject, all their ideas seemed a whole lot better than mine. I didn't feel I had a lot to contribute. So much of my time was setting in quiet desperation, which is what I felt in Dennis; a kindred spirit. When he didn't come to the meetings, I felt more alone on the island. To my credit I didn't want to die alone. So, I kept showing up. I trusted these guys and hoped for the best.

142

Colin

Colin always seemed quiet to me, not a mover and shaker, but steady, always there with appropriate thoughts and usually a pretty thought-out comment.

The first time I really was aware of Colin's presence was when Mike kept avoiding dealing with his issues and Colin had had it. Colin got red faced, extremely angry and blew up. It shocked everyone, especially me. This wasn't the Colin I knew. That day in 1996, I think, was the day I saw the Colin inside jump outside. From that point on Colin was a force in the group, a quiet, but direct, articulate, thoughtful force that communicated sound reasoning. In retrospect, I am sure it was always there. It just needed that atom bomb to let it out.

Since that time, Colin has been a sounding board of reason. He is steady and thinks things out well. His background as a college professor in England was a core element of himself he aligned with early on and continued to mold most of his life. Uniquely, his steady approach to life has been the foundation that inspired him to learn and to teach on a bigger scale. So he methodically put together his teachers passion for learning, enhanced his understanding of the written media of books, jumped in with both feet to understand this new media of the internet and social media, and the journey continues.

What I admire most about Colin is his tenacity to hang in there. I saw that with the group in the beginning. I saw it with his books, with what he has done with his videos, internet presence, and his relationship with JoAnn and reconnecting with Lorraine, his daughter, as well as his other children. I also admire his quiet passion about teaching and helping others. It is the essence of Colin . . . helping others come to terms with who they are and who they can be.

The paradoxical part of Colin is his quiet demeanor, yet, inside is a powerful passion to make a difference. He will drive that passion like a run-away freight train, yet seems to be in easy control almost all the time.

What I've learned from Colin:

Both tenacity and trust to elevate and inspire. I know Colin believes in himself. When he is challenged and things are on the line, Colin is going to work it out. He is probably the guy with the biggest challenges when we started and the most notable success as we have grown. In life he trusted, he assumed his own accountability, he worked, he listened, he believed, he kept his heart open and he lived it passionately. He continues to teach and give direction and inspire those who need hope. What's not to learn from this?

George

If there was such a thing as a patriarch of a group, George is it. He is the guy who was one of the founding fathers, he initiated the group, and was the glue that held it together and kept it going. From the beginning, he must have had it in his mind that this men's group needed to be done. There must be some way we can get together as men and relate on a deeper level.

I don't know if I ever met a guy who had a better memory. Names, faces, events, you name it. He could pull them out of his head at random. Books he read; he could recite passages that he read years ago, verbatim.

One aspect of his personality that has always struck me is how when he said something, I felt like we all listened and most of what he said was probably right on or darn close. But then again, not always. But it was because he was so often on when he said something that was not as supportive or right on, you still wanted to buy into it. It made me want to be attentive to every conversation with him. Yet, in the case of Farra, when George was confrontational I felt fearful, not as much for Farra, but for myself. He could and would push deep into his consciousness. I want to note that this was not bad as long as Farra, or whoever could stay with it, because George, usually, would know when to stop. But that pushing could and usually was very uncomfortable, even fearful, shameful, guilty, less than, etc., but it would also break down barriers.

George had the common thread that we all had. That ability and a willingness to probe you for where is that feeling or attitude was coming from, i.e. Mom, Dad, family member, society, tribal, primal, wherever. Then hold you to it and help you dissolve it. He, like the rest of the group, was tenacious about hanging in there to dissolve it. If it took 20 minutes or 2 hours, it didn't matter. All were FULLY PRESENT during your time.

I have a fondness for George, as he is always a good listener. And since not being listened to as a boy, this is an enduring quality that I and most other people gravitate toward. It is this capacity that is probably one of George's greatest strengths. He likes to help people to facilitate change in their lives and he is very good at it. He will ask probing questions, looking for points of clarity that makes or helps you review what you are, or were, thinking and why you did or are doing what you

145

are. This questioning helps peel off the layers to help you get to the bottom of your concern or fear. This is George, *The Facilitator.*

Gregory

Greg was an easy one to admire. This guy didn't join Corporate America and follow much conventional thinking. He found what resonated within him, embraced it and figured out how he could make it work.

First and foremost, I admire his absolute belief in his connection with aligned spiritual beings. The ones that he channels and the ones he asks for guidance and support. He is extremely intentional about his work and very particular about his preparation, from his diet, physical awareness to his spiritual and mental attunement and clarity. His work is a very deliberate process. If it were not, he would not have stayed with us and we would not have had the insight into a unique realm of our spirituality.

I also admire Greg's integrity. People, especially men in a position of power attract others, especially women, who want to be in that power. Over the years, he has had many opportunities to exploit that position. But, to his credit, and strength of character and solid alignment he has used those situations to elevate himself and others to a Higher Purpose. This strong conviction has given me all the more reason to believe in him and the information he relates to us. Yes, I believe in Channels, at least this Channel. He has helped me get out of my small thinking and helped me see a bigger more reliable existence than what our limited minds have been lead to believe.

One more side note about Greg. He is a survivor. Imagine, if you will, the market for a Channel. If this was given to you and you were clear that this was your purpose, what would you do with this gift? Like many gifts that most people have, if they are not accepted by the general public, they hide them and live in quiet desperation never to be revealed. Like the great masters, explorers and teachers, someone had to be the first. Some of those were shot, hung or poisoned. Some changed the lives of generations to come. Gregory might just be hanging with these guys.

What I didn't understand about Greg was how could he do what he does. If you have ever seen a channeling session, it is exhausting on one's physical body. If he keeps doing this over the years, and he has been doing this for a lot of years, it can deplete his bodies resources.

Things I have noticed over the years with Greg are his ease with me and the group. He laughs easily, is upbeat and has always been there for all of us. I think he is happier and more at ease with himself and being in his own skin. I also see him getting revitalized with his connection of like-minded people, who understand and want to understand more about who he really is. I also see as he strengthens his solid relationship with Sandy his kids and family are stabilizing. They seem to be a new stabilizing force in his life.

What I learned from Greg is commitment, belief and trust. He is committed to what he believes in. You don't do channeling for a living on a whim. The work he does takes a lot of forethought and if he wasn't committed it would have never happened. I also know how strong Greg's intentions are to elevate us and others, and to let us know that we are not alone here. Furthermore, if we believe we all have a divine purpose, there are infinite resources available to us to use if we know how to connect with them. We need to trust that our prayers, thoughts, beliefs and dreams are being answered if we are willing to look in places that were once foreign us.

Farra

What I admire about Farra: I would think everyone wants someone to champion them. Someone who will be on their side and give them support when they need it. This is Farra. Your heart is his heart. He is kind, sensitive and is going to support you where he can when he can.

I also admire his openness. His thoughts are not boxed in. He can allow for and hear other perspectives without making any of them wrong. This allows for a more open flow of thoughts and ideas, feelings and attitudes that makes people feel comfortable being around him.

Oh, and did I mention…he is a great listener. He is always attentive to your conversations and will ask you to clarify something if he is not sure he understands what you said or meant just so he knows he is with you. This is a very enduring quality.

The difficult thing to understand about Farra is his difficulty holding focus at times. He is out there and connected with so many people that the possibilities are there for him if he could hold himself on-task. You know his purpose is solid and he is definitely passionate about his beliefs, but it is his focus that needs the fine tuning. I think he is turning that around, so he is getting it.

148

The changes I observed about Farra are probably in his work. Farra is the owner and director of Life Works, a life coaching school. In the beginning, he struggled with some of the pieces of running his company. What I saw was he needed to be a little less loose about his practice and stay more focused on what he wanted to accomplish. I see that is now happening. His numbers seem to be increasing and he is getting the success we felt he was capable of. The teacher is becoming more of an administrator.

What did I learn? Farra is probably my best teacher. I am an inside the lines, hold to the grindstone, get it done, get to the finish line on time and make sure you looked good doing it. Farra, on the other hand, was outside the lines, look over here, I mean over here, no I mean over there. By being outside the box, he includes lots of people and personalities. He includes others and laughs a lot with them. He makes the game fun. He is more concerned with enjoying the experience than what it looks like in the process. He allows for the possibilities.

His whole demeanor challenged me almost continually. So I had a choice, drop my bullshit control, lighten up, open my heart and laugh a little. Or, try to force Farra into a box, try to make him someone he was not and then lose his lightheartedness, loving heart and his infectious laughter.

I opted for the latter. Thanks, Buddy, for staying true to yourself.

My Reflections on Being Part of the Chiron Brotherhood

by Colin Tipping

It would be almost 10 years to the day since I arrived in the States that I received a phone call from George in November, 1994 inviting me to a meeting at Farra Allen's house on Lake Lanier to discuss the possibility of starting up a group composed of men healers.

I jumped at it. Being married, and the nature of my work being such that I spent a lot of my time around women, the idea of being a member of a group of men had instant appeal.

I knew George from him being a member of the Universal Brotherhood Movement, which was a spiritual organization run by Rick and Jeni Prigmore to ordain ministers who were doing spiritual work in the world at large. JoAnn and I met him at a weekly Peace Gathering at the Prigmore's house which was fun and was a great place to feel a sense of community. JoAnn and I did a workshop with George so that's how we got well-acquainted with each other.

Three of the other founding members of the group that we would eventually name the *Chiron Brotherhood,* were also regular visitors at the Peace Gathering. They were Gregory Possman, Gerry Parsons and Dennis McCauley, so at least I

151

had a familiarity with those guys, which made the prospect of joining this group all the more appealing. I had met Farra Allen only once very briefly at a chiropractor's office in Atlanta. (He had no recall of it.) But I liked him immediately even though he seemed loud and boisterous.

I mentioned in the Introduction how it was that Jack came to be a member which is quite a story involving the kind of link ups that even the CIA and a whole bunch of SEALS would be hard put to pull off.

We gathered for the meeting at Farra's house on the Lake on November 18th, 1994. Besides those I already mentioned, there was a friend of Farra's whose name was Lou and a guy called Wheel. I believe Gerry invited him. At one point, he left to go get his bicycle saying he would be back momentarily and was committed to being in the group. We never saw or heard of him again. It became a standing joke for years — "Is Wheel here yet? Wheel should be here any moment. I think I can hear his truck coming." Farra loved that one.

I really liked Lou and was very disappointed to learn that he wouldn't be a member since he lived in Florida. The group was, therefore, George, Dennis, Gerry, Gregory, Farra, Joe, Jack and myself. We would meet every 6-8 weeks for the whole weekend with the intention of supporting each other dealing with our core issues and the particular problems that male healers face in their professional practices.

How these sessions generally proceeded and how we divided social time and work time, what we did and how it all developed is explained in the Introduction, so I won't repeat it here. Besides, I don't have much recall about the individual meetings. However, I do recall feeling, after the first few meetings, a lot of resistance to attending. If JoAnn had not pushed me to go on each occasion, I probably would have stopped going, even though once I was there I enjoyed it. Looking back, I now see that she knew just how much I needed to have more of this male energy in my life, so I have a lot to thank her for in this regard.

One of the first agreements we made was that every important decision had to be made on the basis of consensus. Given the size of most of the egos in the group this was essential. But as you can imagine, it led to a lot of very heated arguments, especially when it came to the level of commitment to being present in the group. These struggles would go on for hours.

I enjoyed watching the cut and thrust of each argument as each of the big egos battled it out, but as always, being a Libra, I found myself thinking I could go either way. I always see both sides of any issue and seldom ever can make a decision without help.

But, when we finally made the decision that commitment had to be 100% or nothing, I was happy about it, if only because it would force me to attend. Whereas, if there was flexibility about it, which is what Farra argued for, I would probably take the opportunity to decrease my attendance and slip quietly away.

Looking back, it was the right decision without a doubt. Even so, it was all one big power struggle at least for the whole first year.

Not that it wasn't stimulating. It really was. After all, how often do we get the chance to be authentic and really confront ourselves about making decisions that really matter, and to do so with a group of guys who love and support us unconditionally?

That's what made these first few years really interesting and probably quite unique. We had no hidden agendas and no one was hiding. We weren't jockeying for power or position. It was all about being authentic and real the whole time.

Whenever someone got triggered and it was clear that it was shadow stuff coming up, we would get down and process it out as soon as possible. A lot of healing came out of all these heated exchanges and love was present the whole time.

And believe it or not, it was fun in a certain way too. And here's another thing. No matter how strongly we argued about things, it never became personal. Our bonding only became deeper.

For the most part, I stayed out of most of the arguments. It's not that I didn't have things I wanted to say, but most of the time I did not have the nerve to break in, nor could I ever find a gap in the back and forth exchanges where I could get a word in edgeways. Their egos were so strong that I let slip many opportunities to contribute. I remained very much on the periphery of everything, but I still enjoyed every minute of it all.

Amusingly, Farra, being the rescuer and caring person that he is, would see that I wanted to say something and would announce, *"Wait, Colin wants to say something. Listen now!"*

That would put me under more pressure to say something important or erudite, and, unfortunately, that was not always what came out of my mouth.

There was another reason why I struggled about coming to the group. Migraine headaches. I'd had them all my life, sometimes 3 or 4 days a week and I was still having them just as frequently during all those years. I had preventative medication, but it didn't always work so it was a big risk for me to be away from home, even for one night. The sleeping arrangements were not optimal and I did not sleep well most times. I often was in pain the whole weekend. The guys worked on me, but none of it helped. I slowly and gradually grew out of these headaches after I reached the 60 mark, but they had been a severe limiting factor for me all my life. It's a crippling condition when it's that chronic, and it made my attending the group somewhat stressful.

There was another reason why I held back a great deal which I should mention and it has been a factor all the way through for me. This was not so much about our discussions about the logistical issues as it was about the nature of the work we did.

I understand the concept of the wounded healer very well, so being part of a group of wounded healers, where everyone was dedicated to healing those wounds, was attractive to me. I also fully understand the need for the physical breaking down of the armor that protected the pain around the heart and blocked the release of emotional energy, so I felt very comfortable with the Reichian bodywork. I had no problem with holding pressure points, doing breathwork, etc. Nevertheless, my own approach to healing, even though it included a lot of what we all did in the group, was not altogether the same as the other guys.

Several years before we started the group I had developed and embraced the concept of Radical Forgiveness and had been teaching it at seminars and workshops for quite some time, well before writing the book about it in 1997.

The first step in the Radical Forgiveness process is to recount the story of how we became wounded and took on the mantle of the victim. We are asked feel it fully; feel the anger and the pain of it and give it full expression.

That much was the same. It is what we all did - and with gusto. We screamed, we cried and we cursed. The others held us down and pushed deep into our bodies to release the victim story. And a lot was released, I know that. I strongly believed then, and still do, that doing this part and feeling the feelings are an essential part of the healing process. You cannot heal what you don't feel.

But there was a lot of what Caroline Myss calls *Woundology* within the group. Woundology occurs when we come to identify so strongly with our wound that we become addicted to the feeling of being a victim because of it.

When this happens, we then just keep on going over and over it in a never-ending loop to maintain the story we made up about it, forever blaming the person who inflicted the wound for what is not working in our lives. It fosters victim consciousness which tends to spawn more of the same as time goes on.

Please don't get me wrong. I certainly believe it is necessary to access the pain associated with the wound and to neutralize the negative beliefs and energies associated with it But, once we have done that, I think we can avoid the woundology trap by fully embracing the basic tenet of Radical Forgiveness, which is that there is nothing to heal because nothing wrong, or right, ever happened.

Whatever occurred was simply what our Higher Self had wanted and chose to have. This means there are no mistakes and we are not victims. We chose our parents and had a soul contract with them and other people in our lives to give us these experiences which we judge in retrospect as being wrong. At the human level and according to human law, they are wrong, but not at the spiritual level. Once we become open to that, the pain and suffering is significantly reduced and the power that the story exerts over us is diminished.

Now, I fully acknowledge that everyone in the group shared these basic notions at the intellectual level and knew where I was coming from. However, it was never on the group agenda to embrace it and use it as a way to finally free ourselves from our stories.

And I didn't push it. In retrospect, I should have argued more forcefully for the use of the tools I had developed that I knew created the shift in consciousness. But, again, I allowed the more powerful guys in the group to dominate and I went along with whatever was presented. Although I saw it gave relief, I felt that it didn't move the pain out for good. So meeting after meeting it would come up again and the process would be repeated.

This was frustrating for me because I felt that Radical Forgiveness offered a better way. A simpler and more effective way. Once we get it that the wound occurred because it was what our soul wanted, the feeling of victimhood evaporates. No more wound. We then become responsible and accountable for our own lives and we stop blaming others for our unhappiness, particularly our parents whom we chose.

Yes, "Shit happens," as they say. But it happens FOR us, not TO us and we create it. Real healing, if we want to call it that, is when we stop declaring it shit and stop projecting our victimhood onto the phantom we have named our *wounded inner-child.*

However, even though I felt the other members respected my opinion, especially after I had written the book, and even though, with the exception of Jack, the guys had experienced my workshop at various times throughout our times together, I felt they basically humored me over it.

So, for the most part I held my counsel, said little and went along with doing the work their way, which accounts for why I was quiet for a lot of the time. Again, I stress that I was not opposed to the methods that predominated, but I felt there was a better and easier way to do it once the story was told and the feelings expressed. My fear of powerful men also played its part in my reluctance to push myself forward.

At some point, I think it was in the Spring of 1995, we looked at the possibility of opening the group to more members. Personally, I didn't like the idea but the consensus was that we would try it out on a probationary basis.George recommended that Michael join along with Phil.

This was later to prove to have been a fateful decision for me and it was to change my life. In order to explain why, I have to jump forward a good bit to May of 1996. Right after Mike had joined the previous year I developed a strong dislike for him. I won't say why I disliked him. It is not important why. I just tolerated him as best I could.

But one day, when we were meeting at Jack's house, which by then had become our regular meeting point, Mike was going on and on about something and everyone was arguing with or against him. At some point, I exploded and out poured all my long held frustration with him, as well as all the other egos in the room and I simply let fly. It was a tirade. A rant. And, I have to admit, at that point it did become personal. I rounded on them all, one after the other, but mostly on Mike. I spat a stream of venom towards him and the others too, but again, mostly at Mike.

I don't remember how long my tirade lasted, nor even what came out of my mouth, but I see it now as a major turning point in my life. For the first time ever, I was no longer in the least bit intimidated by these men who, up to then, I had seen as a lot more powerful than me. I had found my own power as a man.

From that day, on I took my place in that group as an equal and never looked back. And the other thing I remember about that incidence was how happy those guys were to see me own my power. Even now they speak of it as being one of the highlights of our group experience. If that isn't love, I don't know what is.

I have always attached myself to powerful men but always put myself in a position where I felt not so inferior to them but junior in some way. I looked up to them and found my strength through them.

That is not the case today. As a result of being in this men's group, and in particular through this experience, I found out that I could be that for myself. I had found my voice and I do believe this incident enabled me to go out and speak to hundreds of people about Radical Forgiveness in a powerful and unapologetic way, in stark contrast to how I had held back about it early on in the group for fear of being dismissed.

Changing gears now, I recall that in January of 95, well prior to that incident, we held a birthday party for Farra on the Sunday right after the group meeting and learned an important lesson about energy. It had been planned ahead of time that the women would come and join us at around 5:00 p.m.

Energetically, it was a disaster. When the women arrived, it was like oil and water trying to mix. It did not work and we vowed never to try mixing the two energies like that again. Regrettably, though, the lesson was not well taken and for some members of the group they were to receive the same lesson again but with much more force and with even more dire results. Fortunately, I was not part of that. More about that later.

Lest anyone should get the wrong idea about what I have just said, I need to point out that there was absolutely no misogynistic sentiment in our men's group, neither about any of our spouses or towards women in general. It never degenerated into a wife bashing session. In fact, we all

160

appreciated how much we were supported by them in doing this work and meeting together as a group without their presence. Jack's wife, Jeanne, in particular, was extremely generous and gracious in not only letting us meet in their lovely home but actually vacating it for the whole weekend so we could be free of all feminine energy during that time. We always made sure there would a bunch of flowers for her when she returned.

For a long time, Jack had been requesting that his friend and personal trainer, John, a Vietnam veteran, join the group. It was resisted for a long while but finally he came in and was with the group for about a year. He was an interesting character, much wounded by his experience in Vietnam. It was not a comfortable liaison.

In January of 1996, we had another birthday bash for Farra, but this time we built a sweat lodge down by the lake. Gerry set it up for a pipe carrier named Phillipe to come and be the pourer. We spent all day cutting willow and building the lodge, creating tobacco ties and building a great fire outside the lodge in which the *grandfather rocks* would be heated to bright red heat before being brought into the lodge. There was snow on the ground and it was a cold, clear and crisp evening when we entered the lodge naked, right as the sun disappeared beneath the horizon. The flap was closed after the first round of heated rocks were ceremoniously brought in and placed in the fire pit in the center. Phillipe poured the water onto the rocks and led the prayers.

The lodge was just room enough to hold us, but Joe, being the furthest from the door so he could not bolt, had a hard

161

time with the intense heat and pleaded with Phillip to not pour any more water on the rocks. All we heard was - *sssssssssssssssssssssssssssssssss!* Joe survived it nevertheless.

As is the custom, we went four rounds. Each time we would come out and cool off in the cool night air and then go back in again for the next round with more rocks. Those who had the courage jumped, into the near freezing nearby creek. I did not.

But, I will say this. I am not a good meditator and do not pray. I don't really know how to. I don't have a concept of God so I don't know who to address my prayers. However, I did experience the power of prayer inside that lodge. Every time I do a sweat lodge that happens for me. It's the only time I can truly say I pray. I guess it's to the Great Creator.

For a long time, we were concerned about Gerry. He did everything wrong for his health. He looked rough and we all thought he would die soon if he didn't change some things. He would have great bowls of ice cream and stuff himself with cakes and doughnuts. We confronted him about it, but he ignored our warning. He found a woman who gave him all he wanted in the way of sex so he left the group around that time. He died of a heart attack in September, 1998.

I can't quite remember when, but on two occasions we made the effort to save Greg, being the one to have to travel long distance each time to attend the group, by agreeing to make the trek up to Boone for the weekend instead. Actually, we loved it up there and we had a great time.

The main thing I remembered about being there was that the guys wanted to know what my passion was, so I said,

"Teaching." They said, "OK, then teach us something. Let's see you teach. Let us see your passion." I saw this as an opportunity to reveal who I really was for the first time ever, so I got out a flip chart, took the floor and did a presentation on some part of the Radical Forgiveness concept. I think they were amazed. The guy that, usually, says very little was suddenly animated, persuasive and utterly convincing. At least that's what they said.

Speaking of passion, there was another occasion when George invited someone who had made a study of how emotions are revealed in the face, especially the eyes. He used a video camera to record someone speaking and then observed what changed and when. When he videoed me, he asked me a lot of questions, one of which was, "What non-work related thing do you love to do that turns you on?" My answer was shooting (i.e. hunting in the U.S., but in England it is shooting). In the video, you could see how I really lit up at that point and everyone saw it. That was and is my passion and there was no escaping it in my eyes and face. Ever since then, the guys ask me, "Have you done any shooting lately?"

In time, we became so enamored with the group and the work we were doing, that we had an urge to take it out and share it with people beyond the group. Twice we did a large group breathwork sessions, once in the Spring of 1996 in Atlanta, and the second one in Athens, Georgia, three years later at the State University for a whole bunch of students. There were about 50 of them. The music was loud and there was a lot of shouting and screaming. It was very cool.

At the breathwork session in Atlanta, we had about 25 people breathing. One guy, who was very large and muscular, had an abreaction and, while in the trance state, grabbed hold of Joe and threw him bodily sideways through the air, landing him on another breather. Joe was not hurt badly, but the breather was shaken. It was the only occasion where I have seen anyone get hurt in a breathwork session and I have been doing them for years. We had to think that there was a lesson in that incident. Maybe it was that the time wasn't right to take this out to the world.

Our work within the group began to broaden out and include more sexual issues around this time when Farra introduced a book by Brad Blanton called *Radical Honesty*. It was based on the idea that you had to share with your mate every sexual encounter you had ever had, every fantasy you had, your masturbation and pornography habits - everything. Only then could you have a truly intimate relationship - assuming it survives!

Against everyone's advice, particularly John's, who was still with us at that time, George decided to go for it and divulge everything to his then wife, Kathleen. And believe me, George had plenty to divulge. It was an absolute disaster and the beginning of the end of their marriage.

It was at that point that the group really began in earnest to shift away from power issues towards those of sexuality and morality. It was triggered when Phil Hall laid into George as only Phil could, accusing him of hiding behind Radical Honesty and his disclosures to Kathleen, his wife, in order to justify his having sex with 18 different women, some of whom were his clients.

Phil went on to accuse George of being a sex addict and told him he needed to do something about it. Being in total denial at that stage, George was livid and fought back at Phil, but Phil to his credit, like he was a pit bull, did not back off. A month later George entered recovery and so began a long period in which we all started opening up and processing through sexual issues in the group.

This is when the differences I spoke about regarding sexual personalities in Chapters 4 began to become vividly apparent within the group. The physical sexuals in the group were in a lot of discomfort as they revealed their addictive sexual behaviors, while the emotionals, namely Jack and myself, looked on, shared what little stuff we had to share (which others interpreted as a deliberate withholding of our shadow stuff) and gave support where we could.

But it was clearly a case of neither type understanding the other, at least initially. These discussions about sex went on for a long time. Much of it centered around what George learned and experienced in recovery and was willing to share in the group.

Jumping right forward to present day for one moment, I would like to report that I am very happy to see George in a loving and monogamous relationship with a woman he loves dearly and has been with for around ten years now. This is testimony to many things and I know that what we did in this group during those difficult years contributed mightily to it.

Jack had a hard time with it, though, and one day arrived at Farra's house, where we had recently been meeting, to announce that he was leaving the group. George describes Farra's reaction well in his recollection but suffice to say here that it was fireworks.

Farra just couldn't believe it and just would not accept it. He ranted on and on at Jack and acted out his rage physically. Glass was shattered. It was a real circus. Like nothing you've ever seen. But Jack was adamant and finally left the group. We were never really sure why he left, but he said it was because we kept going over the same stuff and were not moving on. It was traumatic for the group though. Jack did not return to the group until 2007.

One of the most practical and productive things we decided to do was to create a Chiron Brotherhood Mastermind Group. This arose out of our being mindful of the long span of time that existed between our meetings while there was no group contact.

We sought to remedy that felt deficiency by deciding to meet on the phone every Monday morning at 9:00 a.m. for a Mastermind session. We started it in March, 1997. The need for this was not just our need to be together more. It was also about supporting each other in creating a greater level of prosperity. We were all having some degree of trouble generating a satisfactory level of financial abundance, so the Mastermind group was embraced as the means to move some positive energy around that issue.

All five of us are entrepreneurs in some form or another and were in great need of that kind of energy at that time. Farra was searching for his alternative means of making a living having been ousted from his beloved Atlanta School of Massage. George was re-evaluating his practice in the light of what he realized in recovery. Greg was building his healing practice and creating a following in people in Denmark. And, I had just experienced a bankruptcy and was at a very low ebb.

My situation was quite dire in fact. More or less since arriving in the States, I struggled to make any decent money and at this time was trying to make it as a real estate agent. I was lousy at it and was only barely scraping a living out of it for JoAnn and me. She was making some money as an artist doing pen and ink drawings of houses for builders and real estate agents to give as closing gifts, but we struggled to make it month to month. Every couple of weeks we ran an open breathwork session in Atlanta. That at least paid for groceries. So, no one needed a Mastermind group more than I at that time.

I was also in the throes of writing my first book, *Radical Forgiveness, Making Room for the Miracle*, so feeling support from the guys about doing that, taking the kind of financial risk I was taking in order to do it was very important to me and it was gratefully received.

Regarding this, let me leap back three months. In December 1996, George and I committed to meeting for an hour every weekday for a period of six straight weeks. George did NLP on me and I returned the favor with hypnotherapy on him. It was a great experience and, looking back, it led me to make a very important decision.

The decision I made was to completely surrender, quit the real estate work and focus on writing my book, and all the while trusting that we would be supported. We were.

The very next day, JoAnn got a contract from a local builder to render perspective drawings of all his house plans which was about a year's worth of work. It would keep us alive while I wrote the book. Spirit provided.

Looking back, it was only when I made that decision to write the book that everything started to work for me. Had I made a bunch of money before that, I doubt that I would have written the book and, since it was — as I realize now, but had no inkling of it then — my destiny to bring Radical Forgiveness into being, my Higher Self was not going to let me get diverted by letting me make oodles of money. The book had to be written and apparently I was mandated to write it at that time, not before and not later — right then.

But I don't doubt that those sessions with George were a powerful catalyst and all part of the divine plan to make it happen just at the right time. It gave me the courage (and perhaps blinded me to the risk I was about to run), to take out a mortgage on my house sufficient to pay for the cost of printing 2,500 copies of the book, that being the minimum print run that made economic sense. It came to around $10,000. I put my house and everything on the line. I self-published the book in the following October of that year, 1997 and that was the start of my climb to a level of success and fame I could never have imagined at that time.

Anyway, we continued our Mastermind meeting for a while and I found it extremely helpful in many ways. I have since created something very similar to Mastermind but is more aligned with Radical Forgiveness and Radical Manifestation, so it fits better for me and my coaches out there teaching this stuff. It's called The PowerShift Group. There are many such groups around the world engaged in meeting this way and we get excellent feedback from them. It really does work. I also have to say that for me at that time, there was value in doing it exclusively with men. I don't know why, but there was something about the energy that made it more powerful for me.

One thing that did come out of these meetings, which was extremely difficult and painful, was a decision to reduce the group back down to its original size and composition. That meant asking Mike and Phil to leave the group. Enlarging the group beyond its original makeup really hadn't worked, so it seemed this had to be done. Thankfully, it turned out to be the right thing to do, but it took a long time for the wounds to heal.

Although I am a team player and go along with most things, there was one thing the group decided to do that I wanted no part of whatsoever. I could easily envision it being a disaster and I considered it little short of suicidal. The decision was to have a couples weekend where we guys would open ourselves up to the women, in the same way as we had done in our groups.

I was right. It was an unmitigated disaster, and I can only assume (staying loyal to my Radical Forgiveness world view that everything happens for a reason and there are no mistakes) that the guys were guided to put their heads on the chopping block for a good reason known only to Spirit and their own Higher Selves.

That being said, there was, by all accounts, a massive meltdown and it all became very ugly. I'll let George tell the story about what happened between him and Greg, but it was a serious breakdown over which George nearly left the group. This event also turned out to signal the end of George's marriage to Kathleen. I'm very glad I did not attend.

With Jack having left the group, we obviously did not have the luxury and convenience of meeting at his very beautiful house on Lake Lanier, so we began meeting at Farra's house on Morningside in Atlanta. George had recently moved in with Farra, so that house soon began to take on a decidedly partyish atmosphere with lots of women coming and going much of the time.

This only fed the fire with regard to how sex and sexuality was now dominating the conversation within the group, but without Jack being there in my corner, so to speak, I was the only *emotional* present, so once again I was mostly just the observer.

It's not that I don't have a sexual appetite or an interest in sex. It simply manifests in me in a totally different way than it does for the physicals and in a way they could never understand. That being the case, they largely dismissed me as a non-sexual being, I think.

Farra had a big hot tub in his yard and many of these kinds of conversations took place in that hot tub, both early in the morning and again late at night. I loved those hours spent in the hot tub. We had so much fun. We always laughed a lot at our meeting.

Fast forward now to August, 2000. That's when we decided to end the group. George had declared an intention to move to

Highlands in January, so we all felt it was time to pack it in. It had apparently run its course. But the unspoken assumption I think we all shared was that without George being there to anchor the group, it wasn't going to work. So it ended and we all felt good about it. I was travelling a lot with my work by then and spending a lot of time in Australia and other places, so I probably couldn't have attended many more anyway.

Jump forward again to April 14, 2007. It was seven years later. George returned to Atlanta. Phil had had a heart attack and died just one day after having a session with George.

As it happens, Jack went to Phil's memorial service and was, in effect, the representative of the Chiron Brotherhood. That prompted George to contact Jack. They had not been in contact for around 10 years.

The idea of reconvening the meetings of the Chiron Brotherhood was discussed and it was put to the others. Everyone agreed to meet just one more time on an experimental basis to see if there was any energy left in it after a 7-year hiatus. The original seven attended: George, Jack, Joe, Farra, Greg, Dennis and me.

We spent a lot of time catching up on what had happened to each of us over the seven years, which was a lot. It wasn't long, though, before we realized that the light was back on and the juice was flowing again. We agreed that we should start to meet again. We would meet for a whole weekend at Jack's house just like before, but this time only once every six months. Jack was back in the fold once more.

Dennis declared he would not attend further and Joe appeared on two occasions only. But the five of us have continued doing this now for the last seven years and see no reason to stop doing so because it feeds our souls. Sometimes I am not able to be at the summer meeting because I live in England during the summer months, but I participate via Skype for at least some of it.

On one occasion, as I mentioned briefly elsewhere, it was agreed that since Jack and I never had experienced tripping out on mushrooms, he and I would indulge while George would refrain but would hold the space totally safe for us. That felt really good and I trusted both of them to take care of me. It was a beautiful experience for me and I am glad to have had the opportunity to try it while being held safe in the hands of the man I trusted the most. Jack had a good experience too and was laughing out loud for about two hours. That was the only time we did any kind of drugs or alcohol.

As a postscript to this, my personal recollection of some small part of what happened in the group for me over the years, I want to say how interesting is to note how we have all matured and grown over the years. All the old ego stuff is gone. The power struggles have completely disappeared; we have little need for intrusive process work; we support each other just like before but now it is easy and free-flowing. There are no demands or expectations. We are no longer competitive or jealous of each other's success. We are still the Chiron Brotherhood, but no longer wounded healers. Just healers.

My Perception of the Other Brothers

George

As I mentioned above, I have always attached myself to strong, powerful men. In my youth, they were always older than me but even now I look to men who have strong views about life, know who they are and move through life with passion, conviction and fortitude. I have drawn strength from such men all throughout my life. George is certainly one of them and I am very grateful to have him in my life still after 20+ years.

Truth be told, I would not have joined, nor would I have stayed as a member of this group had it not been for George. That's not to say the others didn't have a great deal to teach me, or were not also strong men, but George was the one I was drawn to and looked to for inspiration. I still do.

He had charisma and a strength of mind that captivated me and I simply enjoyed being around him. He was the reason I kept coming to the group even though I was in resistance more or less every time. For me, he was both the magnet and the glue. Without George, I doubt the group would have held together for anywhere near as long as it has.

George is a man with an enormous capacity for compassion and although he was a dominant force in the group, he never dominated it. He is a very good listener and because of that skill combined with his considerable intellect, when it comes his turn to respond he can cut through the smoke and mirror story like a hot knife through butter. But, he does so with great love and respect. He confronts you but never shames you or beats you down. He has an excellent memory and a mind that holds an enormous amount of factual information. His power of recall is amazing.

George is a voracious reader of books and like he was made of blotting paper, soaks up spiritual ideas and theories that span the centuries and is able to share them with clarity and force. You could even say that he borders on being obsessive/compulsive in this regard. If he decides to follow some practice or regime, he does it with 100% intention.

George is a very spiritual person and lives his spirituality. He is also a great teacher, therapist and spiritual advisor and has a great deal to offer the world. It pains me that he is not out sharing his gifts, but that is his choice, at least for now.

Farra

Farra is strong and has a presence too, but in a different way. He can be forceful in expressing himself but is respectful of other's opinions as well. He is sensitive, open minded and willing to entertain other ways of looking at something. Though he craves approval, he is always ready to take a confront and integrate it into his idea of who he is — always willing to adapt and grow.

I experienced him initially as profoundly wounded, first by his abusive and rageful father and later by his wife, Latitia, who basically forced him out of his school of massage they both had founded in Atlanta. In recent years, however, I believe he has retained his inner core strength and has returned to wholeness and balance. I believe his current wife, Marion, has a lot to do with that, but perhaps we guys had a hand in it too, given all the processing we did on him over the years.

I see Farra as a man of passion and conviction and is not afraid to argue for what he believes in. He lives life with enthusiasm and, though not quite an out and out hedonist, certainly seeks to milk life for every bit of pleasure it might offer. He has great personal courage and is as committed to his own spiritual growth as anyone I have ever met. He never stops attending workshops and trainings and is thirsty for ever more learning. His passion is contagious and combined with his ability to teach, is finding expression in his recently formed Lifeworks School of Coaching.

Farra supports those he loves selflessly and to whatever length is required. Though I have never spent time with Farra outside of the group and don't count him as a friend in that way, I recognize the fact that no one could have a better friend than he. He will always be there for you. The way he showed up for his son when he was in crisis was incredible and showed just how big a heart Farra has. I love him.

Gregory

I always was fond of Greg, but I was nevertheless aware that there was something going on between him and me over the years. I couldn't put my finger on it, though. Only later did it come out that he was jealous of my success when that occurred for me. I guess it triggered his own sense of not being good enough and his need for approval.

But even before then there was an edge to our interactions within the group. He may well have been picking up on my skepticism around channeling which was quite strong at the beginning, and he perhaps felt it as rejection - his one big issue. But I have come to respect deeply Greg's ability to tap into the spiritual realm, clear energies and draw upon the wisdom of the angelic realm to help others. I have been the recipient of his help in this way and know its value. He is very articulate and has a great deal to give in addition to his channeling to those who need healing. He is a wise and true healer in the full sense of the word.

Greg is extremely sensitive and has a huge heart. He came into the group deeply wounded by the mother of his children, so for a long time he was guarded and careful to maintain a protective wall around himself, even while participating fully in the work we all did on each other. He went for it totally, though, and gave generously of himself for the benefit of everyone else.

These days he has dropped all that protective stuff and is as happy as I have seen him. He was and still is totally committed to the group. He has an 8-hour drive to get to where we meet, but never wavers. He has also started his own men's group in Boone, which again is an indication of his generosity of spirit, a quality I have seen in him from the start. I love his sense of humor, his wisdom and healing power. Even though we see each other two or three times a year at the most, he is important to me and I value his presence in my life.

Jack

Jack is extremely loving and caring and I love being in his presence. I so appreciate his generosity in being willing to open his home to us as a meeting place and very much feel his love. But, even though he and I are most alike in comparison to the other guys, he nevertheless remains an enigma to me - still. This is, in some part at least, due to the fact that my hearing is not good, and he speaks so fast and softly, and with so little clarity that I miss most of what he says. And the more nervous he is, the worse it gets. Most of the time I have to guess what he is saying, which does not make for clear communication.

Notwithstanding all that, it remains difficult to find the real Jack behind the image he projects. Just like me, and in contrast to the other three guys who are all extroverts, he is deeply introverted. This made it difficult for him to make a forceful verbal contribution, especially in the early days. So, for the most part he remained subdued during all the heated discussions. He protected himself in this way, not wanting to step out and risk being judged. He is sensitive to criticism and judgment and in the beginning was very resistant to revealing his dark side. That kind of shadow work was completely new to him. When things started to get too near the mark, he would go to sleep. That was his defense.

There is an urgency about Jack. He hates to dwell on the past, always keen to let stuff go and move on, the emphasis being on the moving on part, which actually feeds into his tendency to deal with life through the mechanism of denial. He found Farra's need to keep going back over his stuff with his father irksome and he thought it wasteful of the group's time, so much so that it caused him to leave the group for several years.

He does great healing work in his practice, but has a narrow view of the world. He has so much conviction about the work that he tends to see it as the panacea for much of what ails humanity, not realizing that 99.99% of the world's population will never be exposed to what he has to offer in the way of education about health and wellness. I experience this urgency myself, in a good way of course, in his always wanting me to adopt food habits he feels would be good for me. He does it with such love though. I know he wants the best for me and loves me like a brother. I love him too and love his heart.

Dennis

Dennis was enigmatic for me too, but in a different way than Jack. He was a gentle soul, extremely sensitive and was even more introverted than either Jack or me. At the same time he was rather obsessive/compulsive, especially with regard to his spiritual beliefs which were very strongly held and forcefully articulated. His need to defend them and himself was a major source of his discomfort in the group.

But the main thing was his fear of revealing himself, not so much to all of us, but to himself. He just didn't want to go there. He protected his heart big time and did not want to do anything that would cause him to become acquainted with his own shadow. It would have been too painful. And I think that's why he left the group.

Reflections on Being Part of the Chiron Brotherhood

by Dennis McCauley

How I started with Chiron in 1994 is well covered in the Introduction and the other brother's stories. But, besides being excited by the prospect when discussing it with George, my partner at the time, Joyce Oliver, told me I needed a men's group if only because I resented her meetings with women's groups. I must admit I did, and I would sulk about it.

Unlike Colin, who had his partner, JoAnn, throughout his Chiron experience, Joyce and I parted in 1995 after its start in 1994. We had been together since Christmas, 1989.

As Colin reports, JoAnn really supported him in going each time, encouraging him to continue with Chiron. In my case, Joyce was no longer around and Jean, my new partner, didn't have any special attachment to me staying in the men's group.

Like Colin, I had to force myself to go each time, but I did enjoy it once I was there and was glad afterwards. I guess it was the fear of the unknown: what's going to come up?

I think the fear and the resisting got the better of me and I stopped attending. Even though I was invited to be a member again when the group got together a few years ago, I declined. Nevertheless, the group asked me if I would like to contribute to this book which I am delighted to do.

My main reason for leaving was that I eventually came to believe I wasn't getting enough out of the experience for the stress of making myself go to the weekends. I didn't have a partner that pushed me to keep at it. Don't get me wrong, Jean wasn't opposed to it. It just wasn't a big deal for her so it was easy for me to talk myself out of going, but that's not the main thing.

The biggest reason for leaving is much the same as it has been all my life with respect to relationships. What I've learned about myself now that I'm alone after six long-term intimate relationships, is that I've always been looking for love/validation from outside of me, and when it's not forthcoming, or in my opinion (at the time) not of sufficient return for the effort required, I end it.

I'm alone now, I believe by my soul's design, to get that the love I'm seeking has to come from within and to be grateful in each now moment for every blessing in my life.

Believe me, this is a full-time effort on my part to change a lifetime of habitually living in the past or future with either regret or anxiety. So I catch myself over and over again and return to the present moment with my breath.

Getting back to leaving relationships: Four of them have been intimate relationships with women, Diane and Joyce for 6 years, Margarate for 12 years and the last one, Jean, for 15 years. The other two significant relationships are:

(1) With the Universal Brotherhood Movement, Inc. This is a spiritual group in which I met Greg, George and Colin. Farra I met at The Atlanta School of Massage which he owned. It's also where I met Joyce, who inspired me to join a men's group. So you see, we owe it all to a woman! Oh, not only that, Joyce introduced me to Jack at a Wendy's in Atlanta a year or so before the men's group came up.

(2) The men's group. We called the group the Chiron Brotherhood after Chiron, the wounded healer of Greek mythology. And I surely was one wounded healer, my special modality being massage.

I always left everything whenever I felt I wasn't getting the love I needed, which I now know has to come from within, so that's my work now. That and gratitude. I can almost hear the Chiron Brothers snickering over the *story* that I've made up. Whatever, it's my life and this is my story to the best of my ability to comprehend it at this time.

So these are the notes I got in the beginning and then nothing, but I did continue to try to visualize and invoke my soul as George brilliantly suggested (he and I have always been able to trigger each other's insights to a remarkable degree.

Eventually, by talking to my soul like I would talk to George on Skype, I got a connection and finally when I stopped trying so hard I heard a name come forth, my soul's name. So I asked for help to get around the block to writing and finally, on Friday May 16, 2014 at 6:00 a.m. I woke up with the words in

183

my head (this just doesn't happen to me - I'm a night person and don't get up till 9am usually), so I grabbed my journal by the bed, didn't turn a light on or put on my glasses; just started writing like a mad man while it was flowing.

I thanked my soul by name for listening to my request and bringing this through. I was told to write without comparing to my brothers (I'd read George's and Colin's notes they sent me), nor judging myself, both of which I had a habit of doing to myself in the past; so here it is unfiltered; just stream of consciousness.

I was also told to write about my love of healing work from the heart, and how my clients often told me about *the gift* I had in my healing hands. I always did prayers of invocation before all my work.

Interestingly enough, I think George, of all the brothers, was the only one to experience my work one-on-one over an extended time period. Actually, I'm now remembering working on Farra just before or just after graduating from ASM, but I never seemed to able to help him very much.

Anyway, I believed in my healing ability in my heart. The problem was in my head. I rarely could actually feel the energies so my head could talk me out of it and convince me that nothing really happened.

So, I want to ask George what he felt. When I relaxed into it, I was able to ask questions to help clients access and release old memories in the pain body. I loved combining energy work to relax the body with deep tissue (Thanks, Farra/ASM) to go deeply in and release.

Come Home to Your Heart was a business I created with my partner Joyce Oliver in the mountains of NC. Colin and JoAnn came up and did it at least once - his migraines would not respond. My sense of him at the time was of someone who was very intellectual and tightly controlled.

Farra came up and enjoyed Joyce's and my company several times. He really enjoyed Joyce as she brought out the child in Farra, which isn't hard to do as his child is very present.

Greg and Sandie came up to Joyce's and my place in Scaly Mountain, GA and we entertained him and Sandie with walks around the Lake and up the mountain that looks over the Lake. There was a big open rock face looking done on the lake. It was like being in heaven.

Then, we took Greg and Sandie back to our passive solar home and Joyce and I did massage for the two of them, and then fed them a good meal. By this time, any couple is blissed out.

So at one point in 1993, Greg said while sitting on another large rock clearing just beside our home, "You're supposed to be doing this as a business!" So, Come Home to Your Heart was born and Colin was in the picture on our promotional flyer as a satisfied client.

Joyce and I often used to stay at Colin and JoAnn's, Greg and Sandie's, George and Kathleen's, Farra and Letitia's, and Rick and Jeni's homes in Atlanta when we would come down from the mountain and work in Atlanta. Joyce worked at a Chiropractor's office (Dr. Guru Sahai Kalsa) a couple of days a week.

185

We also worked at some of Colin's Cancer Workshops doing massage for those who requested it.

We also would come down from the mountain for Wednesday night Peace Gatherings, and also stayed at Florence Hagel's apartment sometimes, or Greg and Sandie's.

This all changed when I left Joyce in Sep/Oct, 1995. Joyce had been the one who insisted I join or create a men's group as I was jealous of the time she spent with her women friends in various groups and with her sisters.

I tried several men's groups & talked with Greg about it. To me, they lacked a spiritual grounding and so were largely macho exercises. I wanted to get at some real depth with a spiritual underpinning so real healing could happen.

So Joyce planted the seed in me and I talked about it with Greg, then finally took the idea to George who is action oriented, plus we've always had this ability to amplify each other's visions. Well, George just lit up and said, "Yeah, let's do this."

I get many ideas but don't, usually, do anything about them as I'm not an action type - very introverted - I should perhaps more accurately say my action is internally focused.)

I find that my good ideas are magnified/amplified in George's energy field/presence. Our minds and souls interact and flow from one good idea to another. We've had many deep discussions and it seems to flow both ways. It's kind of living proof of the ideas that we are not alone, we are not separate and we are one.

If you cut a holographic film into pieces, each piece will contain the whole image - just with less detail - so when pieces or individuals are brought together the image is richer. That's what George and I do for each other, and that's what Chiron did for all of us. Together we shared in each other's gifts.

Colin says in his Reflections that he attached himself to strong men in the past. I did not. I did not trust men - probably stemming from my dominating father who was John Wayne personified. The threat of violence was always present and here I was a sensitive little boy. He hated that about me and tried to toughen me up.

I was one of 8 siblings - 3 girls, 5 boys, 2 older sisters and 1 older brother who had cerebral palsy. I was the oldest of all but him and had one younger sister. The 2 oldest girls were like surrogate mothers to us and obviously Mom needed all the help she could get.

We were raised strict Roman Catholic and went to Catholic schools through 12th grade. Dad liked to drink each night after work (his tranquilizer), but he always came home in time for dinner. We always had 3 good meals each day and a good education.

I got good grades in school and was smart with a good imagination - too good, in fact. I could envision all the diseases I read about in my Mom's nursing books.

One of my major challenges in life has been to turn my strong imagination in a positive, uplifting, healing direction. And so the journey continues.

PART THREE

Essays on Power, Forgiveness, Passion and Responsibility

The Power of Being Vulnerable

by George Poirier

"It's not the critic who counts; not the man who points out how the strong man stumbles, or where the doer of deeds could have done better. The credit belongs to the man who is actually in the arena, whose face is marred by dust and sweat and blood; who strives valiantly; who earns, who comes short again and again, because there is no effort without error and shortcoming; but who does actually strive to do the deeds; who knows great enthusiasms, the great devotions; who spends himself in a worthy cause; who at the best knows in the end, I am high achievement, and who at worst, if he fails, at least fails while daring greatly......" Theodore Roosevelt

Men learn what it is to be a man from their fathers, grandfathers, older brothers and other male members of their family. From an early age, men are taught that to be a real man, one must be strong, never weak, and absolutely never show signs of weakness.

To show any sign of weakness is not to be tolerated. After all, men are the protectors of family, friends and all those who are unable to protect themselves.

As a result of this programming, men these days are conflicted with crippling emotional double binds, such as aggressive

191

money maker versus compassionate husband; stressed out businessman vs. attentive father; brave protector of family and country vs. sensitive male with a capacity for intimacy. These impossible binds are crippling emotionally and physically, which lead to shortened lives.

When young boys show weakness or vulnerability in any way, they are ridiculed mercilessly by their parents, siblings (especially brothers) and their friends. The minute a young man shows weakness in any way or form, the response is "What, are you a fucking baby"? Or, "Now you're acting like a little bitch". There is simply no room in the development of young men for any kind of weakness. They learn to deny and suppress their vulnerability in any way possible almost from day one.

Just look at the role models that young men idolize. Batman, Superman, Spiderman, Jesus Christ, etc. All of these role models are depicted as super saviors of mankind. Every little boy, whether he admits it or not, wants to model themselves after one of these super hero saviors. Superhero comics, movies, television and even the Bible reinforce these models. Anything less is just not a real man. This is where the idea for unworthiness begins for young men.

What young man didn't have a superhero costume to wear when he was playing with his friends. What young man didn't have a cowboy suit, a holster with guns and a big old cowboy hat. And if he were lucky, he may have also had a toy horse to ride. Riding high! There was simply no escaping this programming.

If a young man were threatened in any way, what was his learned response? Violence in whatever form was necessary to avoid feeling vulnerable. All fear, guilt and shame was either suppressed or acted out some aggressive fashion. Bad ass fighters, soldiers or athletes, were all we wanted to be. That was what defined a strong man. These are the models that would bring praise from our peers, family and country. There was absolutely no escape. If you doubt this, turn on your television. Young men just hate to feel vulnerable in any way.

All this repressed guilt and shame begins to take a heavy toll on a young man. The strong message that he receives is that he is unworthy and not enough. Not a healthy message. This level of repression eventually leads to acting out behaviorally through addictions of any and every sort.

The drive to do more and be more is born out of out of feelings of being unworthy and not enough. The intensity of these desires to have more and do more can never be satisfied. This leads to anxiety and depression. There are many ways that people avoid feeling this anxiety, depression, rage and anger. Everything from workaholism, excessive exercise, alcohol, drugs, sex and whatever it takes to avoid the feelings. In other words, we begin to create walls of armor; mental, emotional and physical. These tools of armor become our weapons to avoid any form of vulnerability. To feel the feelings without tools to manage these feelings can often result in total dysfunction. No man wants to face total dysfunction. It's either fight or quit.

This begins the vicious cycle of suppressed feelings which result in acting out in some form, which again results in the need for some sort of medicating chemical or action, and the cycle continues. It's a matter of time before the suppression strategies, whatever they might be, begin to fail. The self-hatred begins to feed on itself. At some point, the party is over.

The healing process begins when we are willing to start feeling the feelings and process the shame and guilt. The only way out of shame for men is to support one another. This requires immense courage. For men to admit this, is to admit weakness and vulnerability. This goes against a lifetime of programming. Few men are willing to walk this path. However, the benefits are enormous.

Paradoxically, vulnerability is the way through. Vulnerability is the very definition of emotional healing. The problem is' how do men get there from here? What's the motivation? Can men even begin to perceive a payoff?

Vulnerability points to a spirituality of imperfection. The Christian symbol of the cross embodies the teaching of surrender and the vulnerability to life. Vulnerability is an encounter with the unknown and uncertainty. It's being willing to take a risk and be exposed. It's the willingness to be judged, ridiculed and maybe abandoned. It's having the courage to face our unworthiness and shame.

I couldn't have faced this inner ordeal without the tough love and support from my Chiron brothers. We faced these demons together and began to peel away the onion, one layer at a time. I doubt that, even though we were all involved in healing work with others, we were aware of our own shadow issues Like all men, we possessed very carefully crafted masks and strategies for denial. We were shape-shifters when it came to hiding from our own suppressed feelings. We could rationalize anything. After all, we had to survive and be able to function; didn't we?

If any of us really knew what we were getting into, I doubt that the group would have ever happened. The hidden hand was guiding us during our formative years together.

The work was by no means all emotional/mental. As trained body workers, we understood the mind/body connection. We embraced Wilhelm Reich's theories of emotional armoring and the way human beings suppress the energy of their emotional body. As the weekend progressed, the process did not conclude until each of us got down on the mat while the others processed our bodies to release the energy of these feelings. Not much fun in the moment, yet what a relief when it became integrated! The gifts were more joy, love, courage and empathy for ourselves and others. For some in the group, it was an amazing upsurge of creativity that was well reflected in their work.

We became vulnerable on every level; mentally, emotionally and physically. This was truly an alchemical experience for all of us to whatever degree we were willing to proceed. It felt to me like my demons were transforming into angels. Is this work for everybody? Probably not. Yet embracing one's vulnerability in any way should be encouraged.

In closing, I'd like to share these words from Thomas Moore from his book *Care of the Soul.*

"The soul will not allow concealment of the shadow without unfortunate consequences. You don't achieve the goal of the philosopher's stone, the lapis lazuli at the core of your heart, without letting all of human passion into the fray. It takes a lot of material, alchemically, to produce the refinement of the peacock's tail or the treasured goal. But if you can tolerate the full weight of human possibility as the raw material for an alchemical, soulful life, then at the end of the path you may have a vision of yourself of the lapis, and sense the stone idols of Easter Island standing nobly in your soul, in the dolmen of Stonehenge marking eons of time in your life span. Then your soul, cared for in courage, will be so solid, so weathered and mysterious, that divinity will emanate from your very being. You will have the spiritual radiance of the holy fool who has dared to live life as it presents itself and to unfold personality with its heavy yet creative dose of imperfection."

So be it!

Radical Forgiveness and Soul Agreements

by Colin Tipping

Preamble:

I had made the point in my 'Reflections,' 'that one of the reasons I held back a little in the early days was that I tended to have a slightly different slant from the others on what it meant to heal.

Not that they didn't get where I was coming from. They did. Farra and George actually came to my 'Miracles' workshop and I once co-facilitated a workshop with Greg.

Nevertheless, they were committed to their own ways of doing the work and, frankly, I didn't need to push my approach. I was perfectly happy to be there and participate in all the process work.

I fully appreciated the necessity for it in order to uncover the core issues which we had been subconsciously acting out in our lives. Besides, it is an essential constituent part of what is now known as 'The Tipping Method.' I simply take it one step further. Let me explain.

Healing, for me, can only come when after doing the psycho-physical work at that level, we move into a place of accepting

197

that, in truth, nothing 'wrong' ever occurred. That's when we get that there is nothing to heal because everything that occurs happens, not TO us, but FOR us. It's all part of our own Divine plan. Therefore, there are no mistakes. So, everything happens for a reason and it's all good. There are no exceptions.

Only when we get to that place can we give up the idea that we were victimized. And, as you may have gathered from reading each brother's reflections, there was a considerable amount of repetition of victim stories in the early days.

I realize that some explanation of my approach is necessary so my intention here in telling the following story is to put some flesh around this idea and let the story unfold for you in such a way as to reveal the underlying spiritual truth that supports it, as well as provide you some smiles along the way.

The following is a much shortened version of the story that is in my book, "Getting to Heaven on A Harley." You will find out how to get a free eBook version of the whole book at the end of this piece. Enjoy.

"DYING TO GO HOME"

Death actually came easy. Not knowing what to expect, the final few minutes leading up to it had been painful and frightening even though I was only half conscious. Everyone around me had been desperate to save my life, but to no avail. It had been a terrible accident.

There I stood, injury free, completely detached; just observing; peaceful. My body lay crumpled and distorted with both legs arranged at very odd angles relative to my torso, broken in several places. The mangled condition of my motorcycle hinted at how fast I might have been going when I lost control, skidded and collided with the tree.

An ambulance drew up with lights ablaze. "No use, pal." said the police officer who had come upon the scene almost immediately, along with some people who had stopped to help. "He's a gonner."

"Now come on you folks. Nothing more to be done here now," he said addressing all those kind people who had stopped and tried to save me. "Let's move on now — and wherever you're headed, do drive carefully."

At that moment, I had a really strong urge to make myself apparent to them. I was even wondering if I was really dead, or whether I was just having an out-of-body experience or dreaming. "Hey, that's my body you've got there," I shouted to the medics as they loaded me into the ambulance. I felt panic at the thought of being separated from my body. I felt very alone and abandoned.

As the traffic continued to rush by totally oblivious of my presence, I felt an overwhelming and crushing sense of separation and aloneness. I was disconnected from my human existence and yet I yearned desperately to be reunited with my body again. I wanted to go back and talk to my wife and kids and tell them how sorry I was for being such an asshole, and then to make it right. The compassion I felt for them at that moment engulfed me.

My wife, Verna, depended on me a great deal and would be feeling very lost and alone. I desperately needed to tell her how much I loved her and how sorry I was that I so often took out my anger on her. She was my third wife.

Susan was my second and, really and truly, the love of my life. When I married her, she was 27. I was 35. Seven years later she was dead at 34. I was absolutely devastated. I went down fast. Alcohol, drugs, gratuitous sex and other addictions I was a terrible mess and was heading for oblivion.

It was during that time that I began to search for some meaning in my life. Without that, I knew I would self-destruct. One day, a friend of mine sent me a book called *Radical Forgiveness.* I put it aside for more than a year — didn't even open it. Then one day, after a terrible night of drinking, I picked it up and began reading it. I couldn't put it down. That book put everything about my life into perspective for me and my healing began. It basically saved my life.

Even while I was feeling this powerful urge to go back and clean up the mess of my life, I began to notice a strong pull in the opposite direction. I didn't connect with it at the time, but was later to discover that it was an invitation to begin moving towards the light. But I wasn't ready for that yet.

"Hey!" The owner of this voice appeared out of nowhere.

Disheveled and covered in dirt and what looked like dried blood, he was still dressed in a suit, white shirt and tie. The tie hung loose but was still more or less in place. He was medium height and, in spite of advancing years, was still relatively slim. He looked like he had worked out a lot and taken care

200

of his looks. Although filthy dirty, underneath the grime he was probably an attractive looking guy. He was somewhere around 60 years old. Not much younger than me.

"You too, eh?" he said. "Well, you're not the first to buy it on this bend. Neither am I. Lots of people have died here. Actually, I saw you coming on that bike of yours and knew it was going to happen. It was inevitable. Watched the whole thing. Very dramatic. Were you drunk?"

"No," I snapped back quickly.

"Stoned then?"

"No.I wasn't stoned either. Just angry as Hell."

"Same thing," he countered. "Anger is just another addiction. Any addiction will get you in the end. I was drunk as a skunk when I hit that bend in my brand new Jag. Died instantly but it was a while before I realized it. Finally, I got it that I was dead. What a shock that was!"

"How long ago was that?"

"I don't know. Can't tell. It seems like forever, but for me time has stopped, so I have no idea. My watch still registers the time of my death."

"Why are you still here?" I asked, nervously.

"Because of that, I think." He pointed to a white painted cross planted in the earth. It was adorned with plastic flowers, shells, photos and other memorabilia. The name Joseph was painted on the horizontal bar of the crudely made cross. "It's like I'm stuck to that thing. It won't let me go. They won't let me go."

"Who's they?"

"My family. They can't get over my dying in an accident. They hang on to me. They drive by this cross virtually every day and slow down as they go by. They have to slow down anyway because of the bend, but they look over with sad faces."

"Maybe you're not as stuck as you think you are," I suggested. "Perhaps it's your own shame that holds you back. Frightened of being judged, are you? Of being sent to Hell because of your drinking and all the other stuff that went with it?"

"I think you're right," he said, turning his head towards me so he could look at me directly. "I am scared to death of that judgment. I feel pretty sure I will be going to Hell."

That made me think about myself. Though I had been a real jerk during my life, I still felt God would accept me unconditionally when I showed up at the gates of Heaven.

"Let me make a suggestion," I said to this guy who was now looking so forlorn, scared and dejected. "I think you are wrong about this. I think God will forgive you. He understands that you have an addictive personality. You played it out through sex and drink and that's all there is to it. He'll understand. Why don't you come with me? Maybe I can ask for dispensation on your behalf if they give you a hard time at the gate. What do you think?"

Finally, he jerked his head around to look at me again. "All right," he said. "Let's do it." But then he thought for a moment and said, "But not until we've had one more drink here on Earth."

"What are you talking about?" I demanded to know. He seemed to have come alive, hopefully at the prospect of moving towards the light but more likely at the thought of a drink.

"How can we have a drink? First of all this body isn't real anymore and no one can see us anyway, so unless we find some psychic clairvoyant barman who would be perfectly comfortable serving spirits to a couple of spirits, we're screwed."

"No, that's not how we'd do it," said Joseph. "We simply go to a bar, find a couple of guys who are already quite inebriated and leap in for a while. Have them order up a couple of stiff drinks and we're away. They won't know the difference. We stay for a while and then leave. Then we'll go to the light."

"You can't go to the Light drunk," I protested. "God will smell it on your breath!"

"What breath?" countered Joe. "You're dead and without a body, so how can you have breath?"

"Oh, yes. I forgot. But it's one thing to die drunk like you did, but quite another to get drunk on the way to Heaven, don't you think?

"Oh, come on. Just one drink and then we'll go to the light together. By the way, I'm Joe Noland, what's your name?

"Steve Parker. But the answer is still no," I replied, extending my hand out to shake his bloody stained hand.

"OK, Steve, tell you what. We do the one drink and then together we'll pay a quick visit to your wife and we'll give her a sign that you are OK and that she isn't to worry anymore.

I thought about it for a moment. "Well, even though I don't have a body anymore, it sure feels as though I could use a drink. A brandy would be wonderful. And I do want to pay one last visit to Verna. She will be in a lot of pain, but it would make a big difference if she knew that I was contacting her and letting her know that I love her. I didn't tell her that often enough. But I'm not staying a moment longer in any dude's body than it takes to feel the effect of one drink, OK? One drink and that's it."

2. A Place to Park

Brian and James were regulars at this bar and invariably met each day after work. They were journalists and liked to meet up to share stories before going home on the train. At least that was their excuse. The truth was that they were both heavy drinkers — almost certainly alcoholics.

Brian suddenly felt the need to have a brandy. It was not normally his drink, but Wendy served it anyway without a word said. James, on the other hand, queried it. "Brandy? I don't see you drinking that very often. What's come over you, all of a sudden?"

"I don't know, I just felt the need for it. A sudden urge. You're right, whiskey is normally my drink this time of day. I might have a brandy after dinner, but that's not often.

Neither said anything about it, but both were feeling a little strange. Not drunk, for both of them could take their drink, but a little odd nevertheless.

No Vacancies

Brian was my choice, but I wasn't expecting the kind of reception I got.

"Hey, who the Hell are you? This is my turf. Who said you could muscle in as if you own the place? I've been parked here a long time and I don't intend to move out or even share this space. This boy's a steady drinker so I get a good regular fix. I'm not having any recently expired jackass move in on me. Got it? So scram!"

"One drink and I'm gone. I promise," I replied hastily, taken aback at finding another spirit inhabiting Brian's body and thinking that probably appeasement was the best policy. "But tell me, why do you stay? Didn't you have enough of this crap while you were human? Why not go to the light? You could come with us if you want. Heaven is a great place. No addictions. No pain to medicate with booze, just love and harmony. You're welcome to join us. Won't you do it?"

"It's not for the likes of me, mate," he said. "They'd more 'an likely send me downstairs if you know what I mean. I can't take that kind of heat if you get my drift. I'm better orf, 'ere. I needs my drink, anyway and it's not so bad being parked here, except I have to keep defending my turf, just like when I was a barra boy down the East End. Always people tryin' to pinch your place. You'd be amazed at how many spooks want to park here wi' me, but I won't 'ave it, y'see. I likes my privacy so I chuck 'em all out, regular like. Some spooks do this and make a community of it, but I like to be alone. Makes it simpler for my big guy too. Too many in here and he might begin feeling weird and confused. Might begin thinking he needed to stop drinkin'. Then where'd I be? Know what I mean? OK, now take that drink and 'oppit."

The cockney accent and belligerent attitude worthy of any sales-cart vendor (a barrow-boy in England), plying his wares on the streets in the East End of London, belied the underlying fear that kept him indefinitely attached to his host. Brian, of course, had no idea that he had any kind of a spook attached to him, let alone one with a cockney accent. Neither did he realize that he kept a spook nicely supplied with alcohol. He might have been grateful though, that the spook with a cockney accent was fighting to keep other spooks out who otherwise might wish to set up a community in there.

"Are you sure you won't come along?" I asked again, having imbibed the drink somehow and was now ready to move out. "You won't go to Hell, I promise. This is Hell down here. The light will set you free. Why don't you come?"

"Screw you, and leave me alone. 'Oppit!" he shouted, waving his arms violently.

Once out, Joe appeared at my side, looking decidedly cool and relaxed. No less disheveled and dirty but relaxed nevertheless. "That's better," he said. "Let's go visit Verna."

Joe and I found our way to my house. Verna was in a state of deep sleep which was good because I didn't want to scare her by showing up as some kind of apparition in her space. I would enter her dream cycle and communicate that way. I waited for some rapid eye movement that would indicate that she was dreaming. I asked her to forgive me and told her that I was OK now.

Joe was clearly impressed. "Nice work, pal! She was really hurting, but she got the message, I'm sure. How about a drink?"

"No. I'm done with that," I replied curtly. "I just don't like the idea of occupying some other guy's body and sponging off him for something as worldly as a drink. I can easily see that might be just as addictive as being an alcoholic in real life."

"This IS real life," said Joe.

"No, it isn't," I countered. "It's between life — neither one thing nor the other. I don't want to stay in this never-never land. I want to go to the light and I want to go now."

3. The Light Beckons

"I've been waiting for you to say that." The voice belonged to a figure who had appeared out of nowhere and was now standing right in front of me. The voice was male, but I couldn't see his face since it was shrouded in a copious hood that extended a long way in front of his face and left it completely in shadow.

"How do you do, I'm Death," he said in a matter-of-fact tone. "I'm here to escort you to the light." He had been addressing me directly, but turning to Joe he asked, "How about you? You too?"

Joe looked terrified. "Is it compulsory? I don't know that I am ready yet. I was planning to stay on down here for a while longer."

"No, of course, it's not compulsory," Death replied somewhat reassuringly. "It's up to you, but there really isn't anything to be scared of. I know you've been told that God is very judgmental and likely to be angry if you have been bad in this lifetime, but it isn't true. All you will experience is overwhelming love.

You will go through a life review so you get to see all the consequences of all your actions and decisions you made during your life, but that's just for your information and for your learning. You will not be criticized or judged in the least, and you certainly won't be punished."

"What about Hell?" asked Joe, who was now shaking with fear.

"Doesn't exist," replied Death. "It's just a myth made up by people who want to control you by scaring the shit out of you. Hell is something you create here on Earth, Joe. You know, you've experienced some of it. But you're done with all that, unless you choose to stay, that is. It's up to you, though. Free will and all that."

"Come on Joe," I said persuasively, "Let's go together. No point in staying here. You'll just get more and more stuck in this plane and it will become more and more like the Hell you are so scared of. I'm sure it's going to be OK. Let's go."

Death waited patiently while Joe argued with himself internally. Finally, he made the decision. "OK, but stick with me pal. I'm scared stiff."

"I will, I promise," I replied, noting that I too had a feeling not so much of fear but a mix of apprehension and delicious expectation.

4. The Ride of My Death

WHOOSH! Suddenly we were both swept up and moving extremely fast up the tunnel of light. The light was blinding, but it was at the same time warm and inviting. Joe and I were careering up the tunnel at what seemed like a breakneck speed. And, surprise, surprise, we were on a motorbike. A Harley Davidson no less, Joe was sitting behind me on the pillion seat holding on for dear death.

Clearly Dr. Death had a sense of humor. He must have known I would want to go to Heaven on a Harley Davidson.

It was not a long journey time wise. In fact, it seemed we were there almost as soon as we had started but the euphoria I was feeling as we approached the light was intense, more intense than any emotion I had ever experienced in my whole life. I began to realize that what I was feeling was in response to the incredible love that was emanating from the light ahead. Pure love such as I had never before experienced. Indescribable. There simply were no words adequate for it.

Barely discernible within the light, at what appeared to me to be the center point of it, was what I can only describe as a *Presence*. It had no real form, but it was unmistakably *there*. And it was both the source of the light and that from which all the love was emanating. Was it God? I didn't know. But it didn't matter, I just knew that I had come home.

209

"Welcome back!" said Harley. "Right on cue. We've been preparing for your return. The members of your soul group are here, waiting to see you, at least the ones who are back here already, plus other friends and relations you haven't seen in a while. But before we get you fully reunited with them, you need to do the life review. Are you ready?"

Suddenly, it all became clear to me. I had been on a journey to the Earth plane and it had all been pre-planned. As my Angel of Incarnation, Harley had prepared me for that journey. He not only taught me what to expect but had set me up with a number of other souls who would play certain roles that would help me learn what I needed to learn during my lifetime. It was all perfect and according to plan.

"Did you like the Harley?" said Harley. "I thought I might as well bring you home in style.

"I think I might have preferred a death with a slower pace to it," I replied, "so I could have said good-bye to a few people and put my affairs in order. Not to mention some forgiveness work that might have scored me a few points on my return here.

I did manage to check in on my wife before I came back home, but even though she was asleep, I could tell that she was in total shock and despair. I could do nothing for her. I couldn't comfort her. That's the worst part of a sudden death process, I feel."

"Yes, I know, but perhaps you might not be remembering quite yet, but that was the agreement," said Harley gently.

"You and she agreed to do it this way so she would get to feel the sudden abandonment. She wanted to feel the pain of that kind of separation.

Anyway, I think all this will begin to come clear as we go through your life review. At the moment, you are still operating partly in human consciousness. It does take a little time to acclimatize to being back here. When you do, you will begin to recall all these agreements, so let's get into it."

Harley took me into another room which was square in shape but almost entirely featureless except for a very large white screen on one wall. There was a chair in the center of the room and a row of chairs set up as semi-circle behind and around it. Harley motioned me to sit in the one central chair. I felt very exposed and rather nervous.

"Don't worry," said Harley picking up on my fears. "It's not like that. We have no judgment here at all, and there is no right or wrong as far as we are concerned. But there are lessons to be learned all right. So it is helpful to see how exercising your free will at several points in your life either supported the unfoldment of your Divine Plan or interfered with it. That information will then be helpful to you in your next life. Let's bring in your soul group now, because they want to be part of this."

A door opened up in the far wall and in floated about ten souls who took their seats. They were so happy to see me and beamed love and support at me with such intensity that I literally felt lit up by their energy. All my fears evaporated

211

immediately. As I looked at each one, the recognition was instantaneous and the heart connection automatic. The whole room now was bathed in love. I longed to get up and hug each one, but I sensed that it wouldn't be appropriate. Later.

"OK," began Harley. "Before we get into the specifics, let's just remind ourselves about why we choose to individuate and enter into the world of form and duality. What's the purpose? Why do we do it, and why do we do it over and over?"

"Thank you. I am still suffering from spiritual amnesia, so a brief recap will be very helpful," I said.

Harley continued. "The first and most important reason is that we incarnate in order to expand the consciousness of the Godhead, or Universal Intelligence. This is, of course, the very reason for our existence. Before we came onto the scene, there was no way for the Godhead to know itself as the Godhead, since it was beyond anything that could possibly describe it. So It created parts of Itself that could enter into existence and become manifest as a representation of Itself. Little bits of 'God Stuff' as they say — us.

"Our role was to expand our own awareness of Oneness (i.e. the quality of the Godhead Itself), by choosing to experience the opposite of it — separation. Being part of the Godhead, when we each expand our consciousness of Oneness, it affects the Godhead in the same way. A perfect arrangement, don't you agree?"

"It's a beautiful arrangement and quite an honor," I replied.

"Yes, it is an honor," replied Harley. "But, as you have discovered, being involved in this work is not without its challenges. Existence at that density feels very heavy and there is a great deal of limitation upon you all the time.

"Having a physical body, which is essential in order to feel the separation experience emotionally, is a huge strain on you. And without doubt, the emotional pain of separation can be very intense.

"So, when the time is right for you to make your journey into the human world, we first make sure your memory of this world is erased and then set it up for you to have plenty of opportunities to feel the pain of separation. This most commonly occurs within personal relationships but actually it occurs in all sorts of other situations too."

"Does one always have to suffer in order to experience separation?" I asked. "Must it always be painful?"

"It's always going to be painful, but let's be clear about this," replied Harley. "The pain of separation is not restricted to unpleasant or tragic events. It can be experienced in the most delicious of emotional experiences, like when looking into the eyes of the woman you love and seeing in that person such beauty and love that your greatest desire is to merge with her — to become one with her. But it is not possible to do that. So to be close but yet still separate from the person you love is painful. That's why people say that love hurts. You can merge emotionally and physically with someone, but you can't merge spiritually."

I looked over at the soul who had been Susan. She smiled knowingly. I had known deep love with her, but I knew what Harley meant. Even though we, as lovers and husband and wife, were as close as two people could be, we were still not One. Not really. We were still separate individuals and there was pain in that truth. Then, when death tore us apart, increasing the separation, the pain was excruciating.

"Do we choose how much pain we are willing to experience during our incarnation?" I asked.

"How much pain you get is a function of how much spiritual growth you are willing to have during that one lifetime. Some agree to experience more pain during a single incarnation simply in order to reduce the total number of incarnations necessary to complete their service. Others take it a little easier and spread it over several more lifetimes. We leave that up to you, because you do have free will, as you know. It is mostly decided ahead of time, but you can make adjustments as you go through the life experience."

When you have reached your goal for the amount of pain you signed up for, measured in what we call Karmic Units, we schedule you for the Awakening.

"That's when we would begin to send you messages to wake up. In your case, I think we sent you a book called *Radical Forgiveness*. That was the first thing we did, and it sparked the Awakening process in you, correct?"

"Yes. But how many karmic units did I sign up for, Harley?"

Harley looked at his copy of my Akashic Record and replied. "Well, you signed up for 7,500 which was a lot, but you actually did more than that. As well as those situations you agreed to create ahead of time with your soul group, you used your free will to create some extra dramas as you went along. You did a total of 8,400."

At this point, the soul group burst into an enthusiastic round of applause. They were on their feet and began to sing and sway, clapping their hands in unison. Music began to flow from somewhere.

My former AA (Alcoholics Anonymous) sponsor spoke up. "Steve, you were hard to handle even during your Awakening phase. You were searching for Spirit all right, using spirits in some cases, but you created some real problems for yourself, if you recall. I worked hard to get you to take the healing road."

"Thanks," was all I could manage. As my sponsor, that man had been such a help to me during those bad days and I was feeling overwhelming gratitude towards him.

"And I was one of those problems, wasn't I?" volunteered a female soul who was standing behind me. I turned to face the soul who had seduced me into many sexual adventures and experiments with drugs.

"Yes, you were indeed," I responded. "But it was all pre-planned wasn't it? I remember setting it up with you before I went in."

"That's right," she replied, smiling widely. "It was fun for me, but painful for you, right?"

"Yes it was. I hated you for a long time after that."

215

"I know. But that was all part of the agreement too," she countered.

Harley tried to take back control. "It's not unusual to create a lot of drama during the Awakening phase. It can be a very tumultuous time because all that you have ever known is torn down, including your identity. If you are not your victim story, who are you? That's a real problem for a lot of people and it's not uncommon for people to take up their story again and go right back to Victimland. Back to sleep."

"But I was the one who got you to the point of Awakening, wasn't I, Steve?" The voice came from behind, but I knew instantly whose it was. I turned around and again met the eyes of the soul I knew to have been Susan, my loving wife.

"It's so good to see you again, Steve," said Susan softly and lovingly. But even though I could feel her love intensely, it was not the same love as before. There was no pain in it. No neediness, no urgency, no sentimentality, no attachment, no baggage from the past. It was pure, fresh and immediate and carried no underlying meaning. As I opened to receive it, I felt my heart healed. The pain of separation evaporated immediately and all I could feel was pure love.

"Hello, Susan," I said dreamily, since it really did seem like a dream. "I have fantasized about this moment since the moment you died, always hoping that you would be here when I arrived. For a long time is was all that kept me from going out of my mind."

"I know how difficult it was for you," Susan replied, "But what you didn't know, of course, is that I was with you the whole

216

while, supporting you through it, along with your Grandad. On each occasion that you came close to opting out, we sent you energy — enough energy just to keep you going. It wasn't your time yet."

"Was it your time to go exactly when you did, then?" I asked, even though I really knew the answer.

"Of course," Susan responded. "It was what we agreed up front before we incarnated. You said you wanted to feel the pain of separation through having someone you deeply loved die just as the relationship was flowering. So, I volunteered to be that one. Are you beginning to remember that conversation now?"

"The idea was that my early death would happen right when you had reached your karmic unit target. That would propel you into the dark night of your soul which in turn would force you to begin the Awakening for your Satori," Susan further explained.

My gaze went to the other souls in the room. I saw my mother, my father, my grandparents and even the soul who had played the role of the baby who died of SIDS. I wanted to go to each one as I had done with Susan, but Harley stopped me.

"You can connect with all these souls when the review is over," said Harley, rather sharply. "I don't want this to begin looking like a *This is Your Life* show."

The life review continued and Harley showed Steve how everything that had happened to him was perfect and exactly what he had wanted and asked for. That included having chosen a father who beat him and a mother who was too weak to protect him. He was reunited with them and all the people in his life.

"Tell us what happened to you once you awakened, Steve," suggested Harley.

"The more I studied the new spirituality, the more I felt the need to do something meaningful with my life. I had completely lost interest in my real estate business. It was still giving me a small income, but I did no more buying and selling. Just making money for the sake of making money became meaningless to me and I was looking for a way to make a difference.

"I wanted a purpose to my life. I felt the need to be of service to others in some way. So I sold some of my holdings, mostly to the people living in them, for a very low price, and used the money to enroll in a training program to become a life coach. I got qualified in that and I did very well at it. But it still wasn't enough. I wanted to be able to provide some kind of spiritual element to the life coaching process. It wasn't just me; my clients wanted it too. So I bought the training program that would certify me as a Radical Forgiveness Coach. It was exactly what I needed and my business took off. I loved the work.

"You have just accurately described what generally happens to people after the Awakening.

When I was through with my life review, I needed to know for sure whether I was going to reincarnate again as another human being somewhere on Earth, even if it was to continue working through my anger and learning acceptance. That did seem to be the lesson I hadn't yet mastered. "So, what is next for me, Harley?"

"I don't know yet," replied Harley, diplomatically. "I need to check your Akashic Record some more before I decide. I'll get back to you later. In the meantime, go party with your soul group. They've been waiting a long time for this moment to be with you, and you have earned it too. Have fun. I'll see you tomorrow."

With that, Harley vanished. So did the walls and the screen. Suddenly I was with my soul group in a beautiful landscape comprising rolling green pastures with cool rivers meandering through them, brightly colored flowers in full bloom, birds singing in the trees, swallows sweeping and diving all around us. It was blissful.

We sat there for many delightful hours discussing our journey and the parts we each had played for each other. I was still having to be reminded how we had made our soul contracts with each other. We recalled each of our pre-incarnation meetings and how we had to persuade each other to be the *bad* person for us in all sorts of different circumstances. We had done it for each other many times and in many different lifetimes. It all seemed so amusing now. We laughed and sang songs together for hours.

Suddenly I noticed someone coming towards us. He was waving. It was Joe! I had been wondering how he was doing and now here he was. I was so pleased to see my old friend again. "How are you Joe? It's great to see you. Have you had your review?"

"You bet I have," replied Joe. "I catch the next train out to Hell first thing in the morning."

We all fell quiet and stared at him blankly.

"Just kidding, guys," he laughed. "Of course the review went well. You were right all along. No need to have worried about it in the least. Everyone was very understanding about my failings and peccadilloes, but once I owned up to it all they showed me how it was all perfect in terms of the big picture. How was your review? Did it go all right?"

"Oh yes, very much so. It's been wonderful," I replied, "Do you have your next assignment?" I asked, not so much out of concern for his future, but in the hope that there may be a clue in his answer that might tell me more about mine.

"I have." said Joe. "My soul group had been arranging it all the while I had been hanging around that darn shrine my family put by the side of the road. I must have been there for much longer than I thought. Thank goodness you came along and dragged me along with you. I might still be there now if it weren't for you, pal. Thanks."

"So what is your new incarnation going to be like?" I asked impatiently. "Will you be male or female?"

"Oh, male again. I'm going to be born into a family in the Middle East. Iraq, I think. I was a real hawk about that war in my last incarnation and rooted hard for it. I thought Bush was a real hero, at first anyway. I was always for strong military action against the *enemy* and if I had been in charge, I would probably have thrown a tactical nuclear bomb on the whole region. That was my feeling at least, so I guess this lifetime will be about balancing that karma. I'm to be a Muslim and in all likelihood will probably become a terrorist. That being the case, it might be quite a short incarnation so I will have a lot to do to get my quota of karmic units done in that short a time. I didn't really awaken before my death this time around, so maybe I won't next time either. On the other hand, I might. I'm not signing up to make more than a thousand karmic units, so maybe I will."

"Well, good luck."

"Maybe I'll see you in Iraq," he said, only half in jest. "You could get the same assignment, if only to drag my sorry terrorist ass back up here like you did last time."

Note: You can discover what Steve's next and most important assignment was by getting the whole eBook, *Getting to Heaven on a Harley* for free simply by signing up for my blog. I can guarantee he is still here on the Earth Plane working like hell on saving the human race from itself and stopping the destruction of planet Earth. You could lend a hand.

Connecting With Your Soul

by Rev. Dr. Gregory Possman

Connecting to the soul is an individual process. It is not a cookie-cutter type of recipe one can adhere to. According to the Archangel Michael, there is a process called soul rotation in which the personality is exchanged for more and more of the essence of the soul. In this process, one surrenders to one's soul and allows portions of the personality to be released. As more and more of this soul energy comes into the lower self or physical body, more and more portions of the personality are released from the body.

One result of this is a situation where the lower self, the human being, responds to life's events, rather than reacting to them. Each individual chooses the degree to which they desire spiritual growth and development. This can be one of the factors which determine the degree of soul one is able to absorb.

In Eastern culture, diligent devotion to one's spiritual practices is seen as a path to soul integration. In Western culture, distraction, which can take place in a number of ways, seems to interfere with soul integration or connection. Many who are obsessed with a particular focus may sacrifice balance in their lives. Part of that sacrifice may be a deeper

223

connection to their soul. According to the Masters I have channeled for over 20 years, these distractions can lead to a massive imbalance. Such imbalance is not conducive to a deeper connection to the soul. The formula might look like: distraction equals imbalance, which equals greater distraction which equals denial of the soul's lessons.

As one attempts to rectify the distractions in life, one actually moves into greater and greater imbalance. We, as human beings, often over compensate for the imbalances in our lives. For example, determine an area in your life you believe to be out of balance: your weight, your finances, your spiritual growth, an addiction you have or a personal relationship.

By pouring a great deal of energy into balancing this particular focus in life, other areas can easily be ignored. One becomes obsessed with *repairing* the imbalance to the point of ignoring the other areas of one's life. This could also manifest as another human being in one's life whom one is passionately in love with or *serving*. By making others more important than the self, the path to the soul is lost.

As humans, we can easily justify our actions, obsessions and addictions. One excuse I frequently hear from my clients is they have a karmic debt to the person they are devoted to. A client involves themselves in a relationship that is harmful, less interesting, and self-punishing. When asked about all of their complaining, I am told it is a karmic debt that must be repaid. This response is nothing more than rationalization and even laziness. It is easier to continue in their patterns of self-punishing behavior, missing the lesson and separating more from their soul, than it is to alter their behavior, exit from the relationship and learn the lesson at hand.

The Archangel Michael also points out that our soul absolutely believes in our greatness. The soul has an unlimited vision of our potential and possibilities. We, on the other hand, through our belief system and our rationalization argue for our mediocrity. Rather than owning our greatness, we continue to wallow in the excuses we use to keep from changing our lives and accomplishing great things. No matter how much our soul screams at us, we rationalize, procrastinate and continue on in our path of self-hatred, blaming whomever we choose for our *plight* in life. We choose to be victims, rather than *volunteers*, constantly finding others to blame, rather than taking responsibility for our own creation.

Caught up in our mind's story of the way we have to live, we continue to make the same decisions, follow the same courses of action and continue to argue for our limited results and experience. We even attract people to us who support our story, excuses and mediocrity. The Masters on the other side who believe in reincarnation, convince us that if we do not break these patterns, we will simply live out our existence, supporting our broken beliefs and return to another life of worse drama, hopefully forcing us to take a different path and learn the lesson we ignored in this life.

The opposite is self-love. In this process, we surround ourselves with those who support us in self-improvement, a change of circumstances, greater education and, most importantly, belief in ourselves. Rather than believing in our doubts and our failure, we believe that we are capable of achieving more and greater results, changing our lives for the better. As mundane as this may seem, it is actually a form of connecting to our souls. I have repeatedly heard that by getting our spiritual life in order, our three-dimensional life or our reality will follow. I've actually come to believe it is the opposite. As we put our three-dimensional life in order, our spiritual life comes into balance. We connect more and more to our souls, give ourselves more and more expanded metaphysical experiences, and allow ourselves a sense of greater balance. We become more familiar with our inner principals and we become committed to a life of self-improvement, balance and self-love. We de-emphasize and discontinue the relationships with people who constantly bring us down, disbelieving in our potential. We gravitate toward those who support us in optimistic visions of our potential. We surround ourselves with those who are successful in whatever area we have been unsuccessful. We develop character.

One example I consistently use in my workshops is the minefield. Imagine you are on one side of the minefield, hoping to journey to the other side without being blown up. The most effective way to traverse safely from one side to the other is to find someone with a minesweeper or metal detector who can point out the locations of the mines, allowing you to avoid them and get you to the other side safely.

Finding that person, and using them as a guide, will allow you to achieve your objective. For many of us, however, this is not our nature. We seek to accomplish our goals and objectives by ourselves, denying the help that is available to us. Mistakenly, we journey out into the minefield poorly prepared, alone and doomed to fail. We step on a mine and, unless we are incredibly persistent, we often give up, sometimes for our entire lifetime. Our past becomes littered with broken unfulfilled dreams, which we seldom talk about, or do so with great sadness.

Examining a more positive scenario, we find someone with a metal detector; we employ their help and ask them to guide us through the minefield of life with a positive, optimistic approach.

Again, as Archangel Michael points out, our beliefs create our reality. Our guide, the metal-detector-carrying teacher we have employed imbues us with experience, teaching new possibilities previously hidden and a positive attitude.

This allows for a much more optimistic outcome as we cross the minefield safely, employing strategies we would never have identified on our own. Our mentor introduces us to possibilities beyond our comprehension based on their experience; experience we don't have.

As we employ these new strategies, new possibilities immediately manifest in our lives. This then increases our estimation of the possibilities in our lives. Our belief in self increases and we begin to take on greater and greater challenges. More lessons are learned, greater confidence is garnered and greater self-love becomes the norm rather than the exception. Soul rotation becomes increasingly familiar. By now you have identified the minefields in your own life. The metaphor is clear, and you have just experienced exactly what I have described. Connecting at a deeper level to our soul requires energy, conscious decisions, breaking of patterns and dispensing with old habits that have not worked for us. Many will argue that this is an elementary discussion of connecting to the soul. I don't disagree. For many, however, it may be the beginning of a journey of connecting to your own soul in ways not previously connected to. It may also point out that something different, something new and something previously unexperienced is necessary for greater and deeper connection to the soul.

We each have a powerful Master Teacher within us, capable of leading us to the appropriate choices that will help release aspects of our personality and invite in aspects of our soul. That choice may involve seeking a mentor or person already successful in the area we wish to explore.

We do not have to engage in a lifelong form of education in order for this process to complete itself. Five minutes with this person may be enough time to spark our initiative and begin moving us on an appropriate, albeit, unfamiliar path. Some will argue that the majority of us are incapable of this kind of advancement and they are often the ones who will employ a *Guru* in the process. Remember the balance mentioned earlier in this article.

Sometimes, others have to show their faith in us before we are capable of experiencing that faith and optimism in ourselves leading to results. I have seen more than enough examples amongst my clients, friends and associates to believe that we human beings are capable of change. We are capable of connecting to our souls at a deeper level, we are capable of learning the lessons we have come here to learn and we are capable of changing our lives. We are capable of the greatness our souls believe we are. Before you dismiss the possibilities of connecting with your soul, try changing something in your life for the better. Give yourself permission to have a different experience. Give yourself permission to love yourself at a deeper level, connect with your soul and learn whatever lesson it has to offer you. Smile a grand smile as you emerge from the minefield, whole, healthy and in one piece!

Being Responsible for Your Health

by Dr. Jack Winner

T he exact moment that I realized how important my health was took place when I made my first chiropractic adjustment. A patient couldn't comb her hair or brush her teeth because the pain in her arm was so intense she could not raise her arm.

I was in chiropractic school and we were taught that a pinched nerve could cause pain and dysfunction to muscles, tissues and organs of the body. This was my first opportunity to find out. So with two others of my classmates in the room I made my first Chiropractic adjustment, putting the bone *vertebra* in her neck back in place by specifically moving it in its proper position. When I did, the bone popped right back in place. Instantly her pain was gone and her arm came right up, just like it had before she hurt it.

She, my classmates and I were totally amazed. This chiropractic bone adjustment took pressure off the nerves and her function returned. It worked! It was a miracle! Margaret went home happy and amazed by her now normally functioning arm. I began my road to natural health care.

However, that amazing miracle only lasted one day. She called the next day with the same problem; she could not lift her arm again without pain. The original problem was back. My previous procedure had worked before, so I felt assured it would work again. Margaret came back to our school clinic and I adjusted the same bone with the same procedure. Again, a pop. The bone went back in place and her arm again rose without pain or dysfunction. This time it was just Margaret and me. Though we were not quite as amazed by the results, we were still happy this chiropractic procedure worked. Margaret was out of pain again.

That second adjustment was also short lived. Margaret called me back the following day with the same problem just as it was on her first visit. It was then that I realized this called for some more involved and thoughtful action if I were truly going to help Margaret.

Then something life changing happened.

I knew then that I didn't just want to be relieving peoples' pain and symptoms. I wanted to find the core of this problem and correct it on a more permanent basis. In school, we were taught how to strengthen and weaken muscles by inserting pressure to specific areas of the muscle.

I had Margaret come in and I laid a Gray's Anatomy book on her back. I found every muscle that crossed the joint area of her spine that might be pulling that bone (vertebra) out of place. I felt if I could balance all the muscles this might help hold the bone in place even longer. This took me 45 minutes to accomplish, but it seemed right. Then I adjusted Margaret again. Again, her arm came up and the pain was gone. Both Margaret and I were pleased, but not as ecstatic as we had been those previous days.

I did not call Margaret for two weeks as I was involved in school final exams. When I did call, I found a happy Margaret who reported that her arm was still doing fine, but was also pleased to report that the migraine headaches she had had been plagues with most of her life were now gone. She said that was a real miracle! She felt sure the muscle work we did must have kept the bone in her neck in place and kept pressure off that nerve.

This was an 'aha' moment for me. I knew then that I needed to do this muscle work for everyone I worked with. There was more to health than pain reduction. I realized the body was an amazing machine. This was my wake-up call and I had just taken my first step to beginning to understand health care.

Over the years that followed I began to search out people, procedures and techniques that expanded my abilities to help issues on a deeper level. Always trying to figure out where this issue came from and how could we solve it. This desire resonated with my life's purpose. I wanted to empower myself and others to have the opportunity and realization that we can have it all. Good health and vitality are within our reach.

The following years I got into Touch for Health, Applied Kinesiology, Brain Gym, Emotional Mind Release, Applied Nutritional Analysis, Neuro-Emotional Therapy, Laser Therapy and many others. The more I saw, the bigger this health picture really was. I saw when someone had migraine headaches, a bladder infection, heal spur, low back pain, diverticulitis, or whatever the condition was, it affected many other aspects of their lives such as their ability to relate to others and themselves. It affected their self-esteem, their energy, their power, their loving attitude and even their appreciation for life.

As I began to understand how the body functions I would have had to been a blind man not to notice that diet was also, an integral part to helping this body get healthy. I saw the breakdown of the *American Diet* as the systematic de-vitalization and de-mineralization of our food supply. I also saw the over-use of chemicals in our water supply, the chem-trails, the polluted air, bombardment of x-rays, microwaves, cell phones and radiation frequencies, as suspect. The chemistry of the body had to be addressed.

I saw Americans getting sicker, the rise of obesity, diabetes, heart attacks, cancer, fibromyalgia, Alzheimer's, Parkinson's disease, Adult Deficit Disorder and ADHD. Drugs, both legal and illegal, made their way into peoples' everyday lives. There seemed to be an epidemic sweeping America and it seemed to be basically a breakdown in our diet. We were being malnourished. It became clear I had to address diet or what I physically adjusted back into place would not stay in place. The muscles, tendons and ligaments were not staying strong enough to hold those bones where they needed to be.

The next major piece of helping people to get healthy had to be helping them learn about and implement a good diet. That *aha* moment came from a young man with Crohn's disease. Seth had had severe abdominal pains that sent him

234

to the hospital emergency room eleven times. The steroid shots the doctors were giving him were blowing him up and he was experiencing massive weight gain. He knew he couldn't continue this. The treatments he was receiving were not solving his Crohn's disease. He needed to find the source of this problem.

After examining Seth, I found pinched nerves along his spine especially in the area of his lower back, which needed to be corrected. After looking at his diet, I realized foods were setting off allergenic reactions that irritated and inflamed the lining of his bowel. This had to be addressed if we wanted to help this man and stop this nightmare.

I adjusted the spine to relieve the nerve pressure and then we had him eliminate the foods that were causing these reactions. Additionally, we had him change his diet so he could live life and thrive now and for years to come. I am happy to report that Seth has not been back to the hospital. He is pain-free, but more importantly, understands why his condition became acute. He has embraced a healthier diet and now feels more secure about his health future.

I liked what was happening, dealing with the physical and nutritional aspects of the body. I still felt there was something missing. People were stressed out and I could see that was having a big effect on their overall health. I saw how this emotional stress could be as devastating as any ruptured disc or hormonal imbalance ever could be. It was clear to me the death of a loved one could put a person into a severe depression and even hasten their own death. I believed the power of prayer, or even having a positive mental attitude, could curb the effects or completely eliminate terminal cancer. This emotional component had to be addressed.

I want to relate a story to you that hit me like a sledgehammer.

A young woman come to my office with migraine headaches. After two weeks of care, she got somewhat better, but not to where I knew she could be. So I suggested she try a Bach flower remedy. This helps release trapped emotional stresses. She was reluctant to try this, at the time, because they made her feel emotional and very uncomfortable, but she was willing to put them in her purse and take them home.

The following Monday morning when she returned to my office, I noticed her face and eyes were swollen. When I asked what was going on, her response amazed me.

She said, "Dr. Winner, I lied to you about how I got these migraine headaches." She explained she was in a car accident and that the migraine did begin then. What she did not tell me was that her son was in the car on that day. Upon impact, he was thrown from the back seat of the car through the windshield. When he came to rest, his throat had been severed by the sharp glass and he bled to death in front of her.

I almost started to cry. My heart was in my throat and aching for her as I could feel her pain and couldn't imagine what her life must be like then and now. At that moment, I had a flashback to our previous visit in my office. I now realized that she had never smiled or showed any emotion in our previous times together. There was very little life in her eyes or her spirit. Now, I knew why.

Then she told me that on Friday when she left my office she did not go back to work. She went to a park not far from her home. She took out the Bach Flower Remedy and began to cry. For the next three days, she released more emotions than most people would think possible coming out of her. The obvious loss of her son, the emptiness, the guilt, the helplessness and any other emotion a parent or human being can feel for another emerged. She dumped it all out.

By Monday, the emotions were gone. The toxins were flushed clean and, though she was exhausted, she was finally at peace with her son and with her life. The light was back in her eyes and I could feel and see her soul had come alive again. For the first time in our short relationship, she had a smile on her face.

Again this was another very clear wake-up call that I needed. I had to address thoughts and emotions with my patients if we were going to truly help them get well, and beyond that, whole.

Over the next thirty plus years of working with patients, I kept drawing on new techniques and procedures to enhance and advance what was working structurally, nutritionally and emotionally. I am clear all three aspects are necessary and combine to support the whole person.

Throughout the years, I felt strongly that my goal was spiritual enlightenment. I kept looking for the pathway. Was it a specific religion or a spiritual leader, a certain medication or yoga exercise regiment? Was it the proper foods or food combinations, or a specific vitamin company? Or, how about the right chiropractic technique or acupuncture or massage? I tried an awful lot of these possibilities and techniques. I know they all helped. They all added to the whole and were all necessary when the time was right and the patient was ready. At each point in the juncture, if I were ready and open to a new lesson, I learned and moved on.

As I reflect back on my life, the core thread from the beginning to my eventual end has been why this men's group, my Chiron Brothers, has been instrumental. We have all been clear that we were in this thing together. We were appreciative and thankful for our opportunities. We believed we were co-creators of something bigger than ourselves and said, "Yes," and trusted we were here for a bigger purpose.

This, like life, is a process. We are all still processing.

Find Your Purpose and Live Your Passion

by Farra Allen

Who am I? Why am I here? What is my purpose? These are the existential questions we are all abreast of. But being devoid of an answer leaves us in a vacuum.

As James Redfield says in *The Tenth Insight*, we are Souls who hover above and we come in with a purpose, a calling, we make an agreement and then pick the family of origin to initiate our journey. Along the way, we experience a disconnect from this and many never get back to what brought us here for in the first place. So the first question is, what is your purpose? What are you here to make happen, to do and to manifest?

First of all, let's look at *what is purpose and what is passion?*

Purpose is that which connects us to what drives us, that which brings out our will power, our reason to be here. It's what gets us up in the morning. It gives us direction. It is like a compass and we tend to energetically tie ourselves to it.

Some people even manage to merge with their purpose is such a way they become one and the same, no separation. It begins to take them over. Gandhi was a prime example as he was completely committed to fulfilling his purpose of freeing India from British rule and dominance.

Realizing he had to break himself up from who he was to whom he needed to be, he transformed his hatred towards the English by developing empathy and compassion. Later realizing he had to stop the violence amongst his own people, he declared he would not eat until the fighting stopped. He came very close to dying and caused the fighting to stop as the government was afraid he would die.

Obviously, this is an extreme example of purpose, yet, one can see the magnitude and the power of purpose and passion combined. Mahatma Gandhi, one man who coalesced a number of others aligned with his purpose, overcame what was, at the time, the most powerful country in the World.

There are many others. The list goes on. Martin Luther King is another graphic example of one who was deeply connected to his Purpose, Passion and Vision.

Passion is the fuel that ignites the purpose and both are influenced by what occurs for us early on in our life here as we grow up. Initially, I was influenced by my family of origin as my Dad got polio and felt he could no longer live his Purpose and Passion. My Mother never did find hers and she checked out early saying she was, "No good to anyone."

The first person after that I observed who was deeply connected to his passion was my high school football coach.

He absolutely loved what he did and that made a lasting impression on me. Up until that time, I had never met anyone who demonstrated such excitement for what they did. This was infectious for me and it ignited a passion in me which still exists today.

This is natural and the Native Americans used to practice this with a Vision Quest. They would go up on a mountain top with just water and contemplate until they came upon that which they felt to be most natural to them. They were even given names based upon whatever that was. We have gone astray of this as many are looking for any way to survive.

I call what we do in my training an Urban Vision Quest. Some are ready to design their whole lives around this once they gain this awareness. Others turn it into a hobby while others integrate it into their work in one way or another.

The Importance of Finding One's Purpose and Passion:

Without a connection to our purpose and passion one is left rudderless and without direction. This results in diminished will power, lower vibrational set-point resulting in an inability to attract more of what we desire, lack of self-love, alcohol, drug abuse and the list goes on. We tend to seek what is outside us to fill the void. Especially here in the USA, where we strive for the American Dream. Whoever can accumulate the most material goods, money and toys is the winner. Realizing too late that this leaves a hole, a vacuum, people are left yearning for the very thing that brings fulfillment.

My son was floundering until I assisted him in finding and living his purpose and passion. Now he has a great career, great wife and overall great life.

Having assisted over 70 students to find their purpose and passion, as well as many clients over the last 20 years, I have had the pleasure to observe firsthand the amazing transformation in each and everyone who has found themselves through this work. Invariably, this is a crucial journey for one to travel as it literally shifts his or her entire life.

For me personally, the rewards have been huge. I have created a school, *LifeWorks School of Coaching,* which is designed to assist students to get in touch with their purpose and passion and express it fully in the world. They are also taught how to take this gift and coach others to do so as well. This clearly is my purpose and passion as I tend to coach others even when I am not paid to do it. I want others to feel their passion in a way that excites them and enriches their lives.

How to Find Your Passion:
First, look at what you used to play with as a child? What about that turned you on? What transpired for you as you were growing up? What desires, natural inclinations (apart from what you were influenced by parents and others to pursue), excited you?

Each of us has a natural gearing, organic desires and wishes that are unique. Furthermore, each of us has a special unique gift to contribute to others. I call it *deliver the goods.* The first step then is awareness, identify that which is already calling you forth, that which lights you up, that which ignites you, moves you and uplifts you. What is that for you?

Initially, you want to make sure you start from a blank slate. That is to say, apart from what you have been told to do, apart from what you think you should do, apart from what you say will make you money and insure your survival, what do you want? What moves inside of you regardless? What is your dream? What do you naturally provide others already? What would you do whether you made money or not? Who do you *be*? Who are you?

Write all the answers to all of these questions. Look to see if there is a theme; a thread that runs through them all.

What was it you wanted most, emotionally, from Mom and/ or Dad? We naturally tend to provide whatever it was for you to others. Many times it is *like water to the fish* for us. That is to say the fish does not really know the difference between water and what is not water since all it has known is water. So what may just be natural and normal and no big deal to you may, in fact, be an important gift to others. That is why it can be valuable to ask others, especially those who know you best, "What do I naturally provide you?" They will be the first to tell you. You can also look at your chief values since we tend to create our purpose and passion in alignment with our values.

The specificity of your gift is important, as well. For instance, I am most fulfilled when I am teaching and training others to get in touch with their purpose and passion. I am fulfilled with coaching individuals, but I have to say, that training lights me up even more.

As I look for threads, I find that both my parents were educators, as were many of my ancestors. I am a natural teacher. It is in my DNA. Furthermore, I am a visionary and always have been.

This is another clue. What do you do that you cannot stop doing no matter what? What do you do that you feel fulfilled in the act of doing no matter what result you get or don't get? This is where you find your purpose and are able to live your passion. To do so takes courage, sometimes tremendous courage, to do the opposite of what others say or even demand from you. It takes persistence, strength of character and willingness to stay the course in spite of the circumstances.

There are many other clues: look for synchronicity, for signs that lead you in a certain direction, look for what you would do even if you did not get paid for it.

This is a deep calling, one which results in an experience of feeling like you don't even work, you just do what you naturally do, what is beckoning you, what is already always YOU. This we call the True You, the Authentic Self and just being that is fulfilling in and of itself.

If this strikes an interest, a burning in you, look us up as we have coaches who can assist you to find your purpose and, most importantly, live out your Passion! Look for your *soft spot* which includes your training, experience, history, aptitudes and values, as well as what attracts you.

How to Follow It:
Listen to your intuition. I call it the *body-mind*. This is located in the right brain and is distinct from our analytical, cognitive,

linear left brain which is always thinking and reasoning. Become still, contemplate, meditate, go into nature and listen. Ask and wait for answers to come to you.

Each of us has Universal Wisdom, Inner Wisdom, and Spirit/ Source supports us in this most valuable and important endeavor. Allow it to come to you. Discover and uncover the answers.

This is the work we do at LifeWorks and we teach our students how to take others there. Listen to your analytical intellect and say, "Thanks for sharing." Set those thoughts aside and see if they return on their own; otherwise forget it. Our greatest potential lies in our intuition even if it takes a little longer to manifest.

LifeWorks Certified Coaches are trained in assisting you to continue to follow your purpose and passion. They can readily sense if and when you vary at all.

Enrichment:
Fulfilment lies in finding and living your purpose and passion. It is a matter of living your life in the act of expressing who you are. This is true both at the personal and professional level. My purpose and passion are clearly connecting others to theirs. This was birthed in me over the years as mentioned earlier and, thus, occurs most naturally for me. The enrichment in both my personal and professional life is incredible. I experience my wholeness, my clarity of direction and fulfillment on a consistent daily basis. It matters not whether one engages with me in this process and I am not influenced adversely if I do not succeed at generating another client or student.

Being devoid of attachment leaves me free to express fully and powerfully and my business is full of enrichment as a result of that. I experience fulfillment from the act of giving in the moment, regardless of the outcome. Any form of expression, speaking it, writing about it, etc. leaves me full. It's a done deal.

I have found through all of my years of coaching that lives are invariably altered and transformed by this work. Those who throw themselves into it reap the rewards, resulting in financial, attainment of one's full potential, etc. Even those who dabble in this find it to be life-changing.

The bottom line is I am all about finding your purpose and assisting YOU to live your passion. You will not be the same person. You will find the one you have always been looking for. And most importantly BE the one you have always been looking for.

For More Information contact www.LifeWorksSchool.com. The LifeWorks Experience, a weekend transformation in and of itself, In the 9-month Certification Training which, along with the transformation, will train you as a Coach and Entrepreneur. You will get in touch with your purpose and passion, and design your personal and professional life around them. We have a cadre of Certified LifeWorks Coaches to support you in whatever you seek.

Farra Allen, MA Psych. L.C.C. (LifeWorks Certified Coach), Educator and Author

AFTERWORD
by George Poirier

Ours are stories of deep personal transformation. What began as a group of male healers, heavily involved in the New Age Movement seeking a support system for ourselves, quickly developed into something none of us could have envisioned. How could a diverse bunch of powerful male ego's ever submit to this level of emotional processing?

"Men just don't do this shit," was the early mantra as we struggled to understand what had transpired on a typical weekend. These thoughts would be on my mind for days after each weekend. It was the topic of discussion all the way home with Greg in the early years, and with Farra in recent times. It seemed magical to me. It was like an old group of magicians had reconvened to perform some sort of personal alchemy on each other. It was both amazing and strange.

It definitely felt like something *other* was directing our work together. Whether referred to as our spirit guides, guardian angels or whatever, we felt we were not alone. Whatever it was, was directing us to a higher purpose. Personally, I always wanted to know what that purpose was, beyond our own personal growth.

In the early years, we all sought our personal identities as male healers and focused on developing our individual practices.

That seemed to be the purpose at the time and, in retrospect, our individual professional work did develop and, in some cases, to a very high level. That said, as I review today what took place during those years, I don't believe that this was the principle driving force.

As in complexity theory, I feel there was an organizing principle or *strange attractor* that was working to create divisions and discord between us that would eventually propel us to a new level of awareness and a higher purpose. We were unable to perceive this in our first six formative years of existence. We were too wrapped up in own personal shadow and survival issues. These years and the intensity of all that processing was so profound that it's taken us 14-years to integrate all of it, and arrive at a new level.

My own view is that the strange attractor force that was operating on us from the start was *Chiron*, the astrological symbol of the wounded healer. It was no accident that this was the name we chose for the group on day one. The organizing principle was to open our hearts and shift from men that were in service to self, to men in service to others.

We finally broke through our egoic concerns to collectively experience that love and compassion for each other and for all. Our commitment to doing this deep work has now manifested as a book that we hope will inspire others to follow suit. We are all happy, secure and at peace in sharing ourselves and our love with everyone.

Namaste.

APPENDIX
Discover Your Sexual Personality

Instructions:
In each of the boxes below there are descriptions of behavioral features that are typical of the extremes of both the Physical Sexual personality (A) and the Emotional Sexual personality (B).

Read each of the statements and then on a scale of 1 (false) and 100 (true), indicate in the box the extent to which it is true for you, compared to the other. The (A) Statement should be the opposite percentile to the (B) Statement, with both adding up to 100.

So, if you give yourself 75 on (A), you would score 25 on (B) to make up 100, and similarly for all statements e.g. 60 for one, 40 for the other, etc. The descriptions are sometimes extreme, so you don't have to identify with the whole description, just the general thrust.

On the last page, you will have the opportunity to calculate the total scores to determine your sexual personality. Having a calculator at hand will be helpful.

Turn to the next page to start the quiz.

If You are a Physical Sexual [A]:
(Defending Your Emotions)
[1A] You are a classic extrovert who projects your sexuality outwards sometimes even to the point of flaunting it.

%

If You are an Emotional Sexual [B]

(Defending Your Body)

[1B] You are the classic introvert and you tend to fold down and withdraw into yourself to protect your feelings of physical vulnerability.

%

[2A] You are very comfortable with your body and have a high sex drive. You are ready for sex at a moment's notice, and if you are a man, you can last for hours. Sex is very important to you.

%

[2B] You are not in the least bit comfortable in your body and have a closed, protective bodily stance that says, "Don't come close, and don't touch me." Sex is not a high priority for you and you need a lot of warming up and mental/visual stimulation.

%

[3A] You wear clothes and jewelry that emphasize and bring attention to your physical body and your sexual attractiveness. (This applies to women more than men, but a physical male is always conscious of how he looks.)

%

[3B] You dress conservatively to divert attention away from your body and to hide your sexuality. You will wear high neck dresses or loose clothing to hide your figure and will wear minimal makeup, and will wear sensible shoes. Men will dress conservatively.

%

250

[4A] Image and appearance are very important to you. No matter what you buy, the main consideration is how it makes you look. You go for elegance, style, color, glitz, etc. You would never buy a car on the basis of fuel efficiency over style.

%

[4B] You buy cars not on style and image, but on which is the most efficient and best engineered. You will research it to death before you buy.

%

[5A] You crave sex, acceptance and attention because of your fear of rejection, which means everything you do is designed to get approval. You are extremely sensitive to criticism.

%

[5B] You do not much like to be touched. Even a light touch quickly turns to irritation. The kind of touch a physical considers affectionate can seem like physical assault to you after a while.

%

[6A] You are the life-and-soul of any party, very popular and always seem comfortable in social situations. You are never at a loss for something to talk about and small talk comes easy to you.

%

[6B] You are not particularly social and have great difficulty making small talk. At parties, you are usually a wallflower. You leave early.

%

251

[7A] If rejected, rather than withdraw, you will push forward even more, trying to win the person over with charm and persuasion. You become very insistent and pushy. You will not take no for an answer, especially from an emotional sexual person of the opposite sex, to whom you tend to be irresistibly attracted. You can be assertive and controlling, almost to the point of being obnoxious if you smell rejection.

[___] %

[7B] You are turned on sexually much more by visual and mental stimuli than by touch. You are not automatically ready for sex like the Physical is and women need a lot of warming up. As a male, you are not the sexual athlete the Physical Sexual men are. Once you have ejaculated, it is all over, whereas a Physical can go on for hours.

[___] %

[8A] When in conversation with someone you will stand close, lock eyes and scan their face for the least sign of a possible rejection.

[___] %

[8B] You are uncomfortable with direct and prolonged eye contact and initially require a lot of personal space between you and the person you are in contact with.

[___] %

[9A] You crave excitement and lots of social interaction so you are likely to be in the sales and marketing business and/or indulge in very physical sports, especially team sports.

[___] %

[9B] You like your alone time and avoid team sports. You excel at individual sports that require rigorous training and are self-challenging.

[___] %

[10A]You are less concerned about your body being hurt than you are about having your feelings
crushed.

%

[10B] You feel your feelings inwardly and process
them mentally. You seldom express feelings outwardly and do not like to show physical affection
in public.

%

[11A] You experience your emotion physically rather
than mentally, and when your feelings are hurt, you
feel it as intense pain in your body. The pain can be
so bad that you can literally be incapacitated by it
for long periods of time.

%

[11B] You lead with your mind in everything, from
work, games and even sex. You are analytical, careful and methodical and therefore seldom spontaneous.

%

[12A] When a relationship ends you are devastated
and have a very difficult time letting go of it. You take
it very personally and feel utterly rejected. You also
have a very hard time replacing. It may be many
months before you will have another serious relationship though you will likely have plenty of sex in
the meanwhile. You need it just to feel OK.

%

[12B] When a relationship ends you get over it in a
matter of days and replace easily. You do not take
it as a personal rejection of yourself.

%

[13A] You are hopelessly idealistic about love and relationships and very romantically inclined. Once in a relationship you tend to be loyal and monogamous. At the same time, you are very jealous and possessive.

%

[13B] You often have extramarital affairs and think little of it because you do not equate love with sex as does the Physical. You like the mental excitement of an affair.

%

[14A] You enjoy children and are very strong on family. You put family and/or relationships before career or any other aspect of life. It's your #1 priority.

%

[14B] For you, (after the honeymoon period), sex is not a high priority, neither is family, children or relationships. Your priority is work and career, followed by your hobby. Relationships come a distant third. You are not very fond of children and you may have chosen never to marry.

%

[14A] You are a natural risk taker in all aspects of your life, so you are likely to be an entrepreneur and/or indulge in very physical and challenging sports, especially team sports.

%

[14B] If you go into business for yourself, you are likely to be an accountant, computer programmer, engineer, researcher, or a technician. You like precise, solitary work and are detail oriented. You can be very successful in business.

%

[15A] You communicate by indirect implication and inferences, relying on the listener to make the correct interpretation. On the other hand, you hear only what is said literally and don't pick up on inferences. People have to be explicit in what they say to you and partners have to tell you explicitly and frequently that they love you. You will not infer that you do just because they are there.

%

[15B] You pick up on inferences and subtle implications, but you speak very directly and precisely. You don't waste words and are not physically expressive.

%

Now add up all the numbers in the **A** boxes and divide by 15 to see, as a percentage, the extent to which you conform to the Physical Sexual personality versus the Emotional.

Then add up all the numbers in the **B** boxes and divide by 15 to see the extent to which you conform to the Emotional Sexual personality versus the Physical.

Your % Physical Sexuality

Your % Emotional Sexuality

Refer back to Chapter Two for some hints about how to interpret these numbers and to find out how this might be affecting your current relationship and/or those you've had in the past.

[This quiz is also part of an online program called *Expanding in Love* which is all about being able to assess, improve and

255

renegotiate your current relationship, or define the one you wish to manifest in the future. The program is based on my book, *Expanding into Love,* both of which are available at ***www.radicalforgiveness.com.]***

You might suggest your partner do the quiz as well. If he/she is not willing to do it, score it yourself based on your observations. It will tell you a lot about your relationship. It is normal for partners to be opposite types, but if you are both at the extreme ends, you might well be in trouble. You won't have enough of the other type in you to be able to understand your partner's behavior. Should this be the case, you may need to get some coaching, attend a workshop with me or do the online program.

What you might also do to get a better picture of who you are in this regard, is to go through the quiz again, but this time give the responses you would have made much earlier in your life when you were a lot younger or before you started working on yourself. It is likely that back then you would have been more towards either extreme, like 75/25 or even higher, whereas now you might be around 60/40. To use our group as an example, the guys would have scored a lot differently when we first started the group 20 years ago than now.

So, the extent to which your score from way back differs from your current score may indicate how much work you have done on yourself, either to overcome your fear of rejection and/or your fear of intimacy.

CPSIA information can be obtained at www.ICGtesting.com
Printed in the USA
BVOW04s1701050115

381999BV00002B/2/P